The Spiritual Dimensions of

Healing Addictions

by Donna Cunningham, MSW

and Andrew Ramer

Cassandra Press
San Rafael, CA. 94915

CASSANDRA PRESS
P.O. BOX 868
SAN RAFAEL, CA. 94915

Printed in the United States of America

First printing 1988

ISBN 0-9615875-5-5

Library of Congress Catalogue Card Number 88-070719

The use of the material described in this text is not meant to replace the services of a physician who should always be consulted for any condition requiring his or her aid.

TABLE OF CONTENTS

ACKNOWLEDGMENTS

This book is dedicated to Nora, who
was so much a part of the process as to
be a third partner. She tested the material,
courageously confronted herself, recruited
other addicts, and typed several versions of
the manuscript. It is also dedicated to all
the countless others, necessarily anonymous,
who have worked with us over the years,
sharing their experiences, their pain, their
recovery, their growth, and their wisdom
with us.

ii

PREFACE

DONNA CUNNINGHAM, MSW, is a licensed therapist of 20 years experience whose specialty is addicted people and their families. She has used the processes outlined in this book in group and individual sessions with recovering alcoholics, adult children of alcoholics, and other addicted people. She is also an internationally recognized astrologer with several books and over 100 articles to her credit. Her first book, *An Astrological Guide to Self-Awareness*, has been translated into several foreign languages. Her second book, *Being a Lunar Type In a Solar World*, was cited by *Horoscope Magazine* as "easily one of the more important astrology books to emerge so far in the l980's." Her third book, *Healing Pluto Problems*, is already in its second printing and first foreign language translation. During 1988, four additional books will be released; three of them, including this one, are by Cassandra Press.

ANDREW RAMER is a writer, artist, and healer. He has a degree in religious studies from the University of California, Berkeley, and is a graduate of the Swedish Institute of Massage in New York. His column on past lives has appeared regularly in *Astrology Guide Magazine* since 1982. A book of his stories and drawings, *Little Pictures*, was released by Ballantine Books/Available Press in early 1988. He has been channeling for ten years. For the past five years, he has been doing body work at the Plaza Center for the Healing Arts, in Brooklyn, N.Y., a group practice with a strong focus on working with recovering addicts.

Together Andrew and Donna have also produced a booklet and tape on healing chants with an astrological basis called *A Solar System Of Healing Chants*. It is available from R.K.M. Publishing, Box 23042, Euclid, Ohio, 44123.

INTRODUCTION

There's an epidemic of addictions in the world at this point in our spiritual evolution. In the United States alone, it is conservatively estimated that there are over 10 million alcoholics, 5-10 million pill abusers, 70 million who are more than 30 pounds overweight, and at least 200,000 heroin addicts. Some 26% of the population over age17 smoke cigarettes. Some 23% have used marijuana—and 64% of those between the ages of 18 and 25 have done so. Many of us have several addictions—drinking, smoking, and eating more sugar than is healthy. Families are affected too. For example, there are 40 million people who are mates and children of alcoholics.

We all live out our lives on four planes, as mental, emotional, physical, and spiritual beings. There are numerous programs, clinics, and therapies which deal with healing addictions on the mental, emotional, and physical planes. This book is not meant to supplant or replace any of those approaches, but to add something for the spiritual side of our being. If we exist as fourfold creatures, our healing must go on in a fourfold way also. We see this book as a spiritual adjunct to the many excellent treatment programs existing already, from the Twelve-Step anonymous programs to medical detoxification clinics. This book is meant to be a personal spiritual tool for reconnecting to the spiritual aspects of yourself, from which chemical addictions have disconnected you from your Core Self, and from the Spirit that created us all.

We began this book several years ago. Donna's work as an astrologer and therapist and Andrew's work as a healer and channeler brought us in touch with many people struggling to deal with their own addictive problems. We had both read and worked with the techniques created by the Simontons in their work with cancer, and we felt it was time to create a similar system for dealing with the problems of our addictive clients and ourselves.

The material in this book comes from several different sources. Some of it comes from the authors' personal experience, research, and reading. Much of it, however, comes from channeled sources, received over a period of several years. Often the material was given to us by specific guides, who are in a sense the co-authors, if not the true authors, of this book, though their names don't appear on the cover. A good deal of the information and exercises came from a usually nameless collective of discarnate guides who are much concerned with human health and evolution, as an outgrowth of their own spiritual work. The specific guides who worked with Andrew and Donna, known as Tayarti, Nindinak, and Arrasu, were often the hosts of other, numerous co-authors. As you yourself become increasingly open to these frequencies, you may find yourself tapping into these same sources for guidance and information.

One guide in particular, Red Feather, of Native American background, provided us with companionship and wisdom as we moved toward the completion of this book. His sorrow at the suffering of his own people, of humanity, and of the planet was transmitted to both Andrew and Donna. This palpable sorrow encourages us to create the sorts of global healing necessary so that genocide, poverty, and despair no longer drive people into addiction. Addiction is not an isolated phenomenon, in spite of the ways we've written about it. Addiction has its roots in the cultural imbalances that surround us at all times. The healing of addictions cannot be separated from the continuing struggle to create global healing.

It's easy to point a finger at the individual addicts and blame them for their addictions, but we are part of a collective organism and in our cycles of incarnation must learn collective lessons. Addiction is a matter that concerns all human beings, from addicts themselves to their families to the rest of the world. To point a finger and detach from the problem is part of the problem. Addiction will not go away until we all understand this and work to change the conditions that make it so.

It's easy to blame yourself or someone else for your addiction to coffee, sugar, alcohol, or drugs. It's easy to feel guilty about the years wasted as an addict, the pain inflicted on yourself and on others, the damage done to your body and perhaps to someone else's. It's easy to feel that you'll never change, never be healed. It's easy to feel sorry for yourself or enraged. It's easy to feel that you're wrong and in need of being punished. We do not deny the reality of such feelings, but we come at them from a slightly different direction. In order to be healed on the spiritual plane, you need to come to a place of forgiveness and love. You cannot get there if you stay in those negative places. If you're addicted to a substance, that's punishment enough in itself, so put aside guilt, resentment, blame, punishment, and rage.

There are many tools for healing, many tools for transformation. When the parents of a friend of ours separated, his father took the tool box with him when he moved out. His mother, wanting to fix up the house, went out and bought new pictures, but there was no hammer to hang them up with. Our friend used one of his mother's black high-heeled shoes to hammer the nails. It worked, but it wasn't the right tool.

Addiction is like that. You know something in your life needs to be fixed or changed. You reach out for a tool to do it with, so you pick up coffee, sugar, a drink, or some drugs. The impulse is good but the tool isn't right. It may work for a while, but in the end, a hammer is a hammer and a shoe is a shoe. You can hammer nails with a shoe, but you cannot pull them out again. Addictive substances are power tools. They aren't the best ones to do the job, but sometimes, like our friend's high-heeled shoe hammer, they are the only ones available. You can get high for a while and feel good, but once that substance is stuck in you, you cannot get it out. Chemical tools are one-way tools, but there are other tools, spiritual tools we'll share with you. Tools that can hammer nails in and pull them out.

As we evolve spiritually and learn to use mind, body, and spirit more effectively, the kinds of tools we resort to will change. In ancient times, the natural organic tools our ancestors found around them worked well to further consciousness. In the future, we will again find that simple tools serve us best. In place of manufactured drugs and alcohol, we'll see our descendants using crystals and plant and gem essences. They will also use simple tools of mind, such as visualization, meditation, and light, as well as technological devices that are nonintrusive and nonaddictive. With these tools, they will move into expand- ed or altered states of consciousness.

Some of these tools are ancient and being rediscovered again, so they are available to us now. Others are pieces of as yet unimaginable future technology. In time, no one will need any power tools but their own bodies and minds to effect transformation. To that end, this book is created, to foster the movement away from substances that damage the body as they alter consciousness, movement toward tools that honor the body and do the job better.

It isn't true that addictive substances are entirely evil. In addition to reminding you of the postive impulses that might have led you toward your addiction, we will often be speaking of the positive functions and right use of these substances as well. Nothing exists that is purely good or purely evil, so addictive substances are capable of generat- ing both positive and negative experiences on many levels. The breakup of a love relationship that devastates your life may later turn out to have been, on another level, exactly the experience you needed to get you out of places you're stuck in and into new and more nurturing places. So, too, with addictive substances that may cause damage on one level and healing on others.

We do not advocate that you look for negative experiences as teachers. There is a name for that school of spiritual learning—masochism. Besides, those experiences seem to find us without our looking for them. But we mention the positive aspects of addictive substances so you can understand what impelled you to seek them out in the first place. Then you can honor the part of yourself which was wise enough to understand what tools you were looking for and support that part of you that is now able to make better choices in life's floating hardware store.

We speak about addiction here, but the book was written

to cover a wide range of individuals. Some people abuse substances without actually being addicted, while others are chemically dependent and yet not physically addicted. The exercises and processes in the book are as valid for cookie bingers and six-cup-a-day coffee drinkers, for weekly pot smokers, and for nightly wine drinkers as they are for people who get called addicts. Donna has also used them to help a variety of other people in need of healing—children of alcoholics or of other dysfunctional families, those who are severely depressed, or those who have suffered from physical or sexual abuse.

The first step to healing addiction on a mental, physical, or emotional plane is different, but on a spiritual plane, the first step in healing yourself of your addiction is to go back to the part of yourself that was looking for a tool to change your life. Say to it, "I honor the part of me that is capable of making changes in my life. I embrace the part of me that reaches out for new tools." If you're used to feeling guilty, angry, or blaming yourself for the addiction and the years it seems you wasted, it may be hard for you to say, "The impulse to use a chemical tool to change a life problem was a valid one." It may be hard to accept and bring love into that part of yourself. But in order to make a spiritual healing of your addictive patterns, you'll need to do that.

The way we think and feel is conditioned by habits. After we learn to tie our shoes, we do it the same way again and again, never thinking about it, just doing it. One way of healing is to reshape our thoughts. Using affirmations is an excellent way to do that. Sit quietly and try these two statements: "I embrace the part of me that is capable of making changes in my life. I embrace the part of me that reaches out for new tools." Say it over several times. Say it softly to yourself, and say it aloud. How does it feel? Can you allow it into yourself, to reprogram your thoughts, or do you resist it?

There's a very successful—and quite practical—prior example of using information such as this book. It's not generally known, not even to the majority of its members, but the inspiration for Alcoholics Anonymous came from a spiritual experience by its founder, Bill Wilson. The biography, *Bill Wilson* describes his total despair at his inability to stop the drinking which was destroying his mind and body. In his hospital room, Bill cried out for a sign of God's existence, and the room filled with a great white light. He got the sense of a spiritual being of great perfection and was filled with peace and a profound awareness that God was in everything and that he was one with God. After this spiritual awakening, Wilson never drank again.   He went on to found A.A., an organization based on spiritual principles which has helped hundreds of thousands of alcoholics to recover.[1]

The realm Wilson glimpsed in his transformational experience is a spiritual reality beyond the limits of what we know in our daily lives. It is a realm of pure consciousness which is not bound by time and space as we know them. A major reason for the current epidemic of addictions is that most of us have lost our connection with this spiritual reality. We have become too mechanized, too rational, too busy, and too frightened to spend time meditating and connecting with our Core Selves. For many, churches no longer answer the need we all have for this connection. We come to fear our inner vision of the greater reality and to shut it off in various ways, of which addiction is a major one.

We can see the wish for spiritual attunement in the very words an addict uses—"I want to get high." This term is a reflection of the state of consciousness achieved naturally and safely by regular practice of a spiritual discipline like meditation or chanting. By using a chemical substance, one can sometimes induce the same state of ecstasy. The difference is that the spiritual discipline is grounded in reality and often has the guidance and protection of some group or teacher. The chemical high is dependent on the transitory nature of the chemical, which drops the energy downward as it wears off, leaving the person feeling powerlessness, rage, and sexual frustration. The end result of repeated reliance on chemical highs is always a spiritual and emotional low and a sense of being in the depths, in darkness, away from the light.

In seeking the high, the substance abuser retains an in-born sense of that reality, but pursues it from the wrong direction, expecting something from the outside to make the feeling happen. The feeling of a high must come from the inside, over a long period of work and conscious understanding. It will not come in any enduring way from anything you can buy, but when it comes from the inside, it is timeless and priceless.

It's a main thesis of this book that we're all far greater than the self we know. There are other planes and other states of awareness besides ordinary waking consciousness. That part of yourself which is far greater than the small, fearful being we know as "me" is immortal. Some call it the soul or the Higher Self; in this book we call it the Core Self. You may very well come to experience the Core Self and those other states of awareness, in the course of reading this book and working with the material, as part of your recovery from addiction.

It's our belief (and that of many people on the spiritual path) that the Core Self exists beyond the boundaries of birth and death. It had conscious participation in planning the life history of the individual before birth. It seeks a variety of experiences with which to learn and develop itself to the highest extent possible. Addiction may be one of those experiences, as we'll see later on. The Core Self selects a particular set of parents, a locale, and a group of events—some quite painful—which will further its total development. It agrees on a set of tasks to perform and skills to master which will be its personal contribution to the world. We all retain a dim memory of that set of life tasks which we refer to here as your personal vision.

In group and individual sessions with recovering addicts, some of whom you will meet in the pages of this book, we worked with the channeled material we had been given and with meditations and visualizations. This material is the outgrowth of that work. We offer it to you, not as THE answer to the problem of healing addictions, but as one aspect of the answer. We encourage you to reach out to other aspects of healing and wish you joy and health on your transformational journey.

This book is the first book of a two-part guide to healing addictions. You will be introduced to your basic healing tools: the power of the mind, flower essences, gem elixirs, guided meditations with color, and crystals. You will get a basic understanding of the spiritual meaning of addictions in general. You will make a beginning toward cleansing your body, mind, and emotions of addictive patterns which are common to people who are addicted to various substances. In the second book, however, you will learn about the spiritual patterns beneath addictions to specific substances and the specific tools needed to heal them. There will be chapters about alcohol, pot, cocaine, heroin, and the synthetic drugs, as well as sugar, tobacco, and coffee. You will also find information on the subtle bodies and the chakras as well as information on how past lives can contribute to addiction. Some of the information about these addictions and the collective urges and needs behind their waxing and waning in popularity will suprise you as it has surprised us. You will make a great beginning toward healing your addictive patterns through the work in this book, but we highly recommend that you also work with the second book to clear out patterns related to your specific substance or substances.

Welcome to the adventure of discovering the spiritual realm and how it interplays with your addiction. Treat yourself gently and go slowly through the process. You'll be stronger in the end than you were before your addiction, because you will tackle not only many of the problems the addiction created, but also many of the fears that brought you to the addiction in the first place.

1 Robert Thomsen, *Bill Wilson,* (N. Y: Harper and Row, 1979).

CHAPTER ONE

WHAT IS ADDICTION?

We are a culture of addicts, and a culture in which it is popular to look down our noses at addicts, not recognizing the addictiveness we all have. Even among those who recognize that they have a problem, there is a tendency to point a finger at other addicts and say, "But look at him. My drug is not as bad as his." For example, alcohol addicts often look down their noses at those who use pills—and vice versa. You who are sugar or alcohol abusers may be highly insulted to find yourselves referred to as addicts, yet alcohol is only a drug in liquid form and sugar can be as much of an addiction as any other and create just as much misery. Even coffee can be a powerful stimulant, and some people abuse that, so we will devote a whole chapter to it in the second book in this series.

When Does a Habit Become an Addiction?

There's a lot of quibbling about who is and who isn't an addict. After all, a lot is at stake—we might have to recognize that we are all addicts of one sort or another. Nonetheless, it is useful to distinguish between the individual who is psychologically dependent on one or more substances and the one who has a physical addiction which would result in withdrawal sickness.

The psychologically dependent individual is one who cannot make it through the day without the substance, who "needs it to unwind" or who, even where there is not a daily habit, looks forward to getting high or bombed on weekends as a major form of recreation. The substance is used to push down unpleasant emotions like anxiety, sadness, or anger, and may be resorted to so quickly that the person doesn't even know those emotions are present.

The derivation of the word addiction helps us answer the question of who is an addict. *The American Heritage Dictionary of The English Language* says it comes from the Latin word Addictus, which means "given over," meaning one awarded to another as a slave.[1] Thus the idea of being a slave is recognized somewhere in the collective unconscious as inherent to addiction. An addict is someone who is enslaved by the substance. We're also going to find, as we consider the history of various addictions, that the very long shadows of slavery and other forms of oppression and domination have been intrinsically related to the development of the social problem of addiction.

In A.A., they talk about an invisible line that you cross over in order to become an alcoholic. It's invisible because the process of addiction is so slow and insidious that you don't notice when it happens. Thus, the person who is psychologically dependent today can become physically addicted somewhere along the line. How soon addiction comes about varies with the substance. Working with the material in this book can help you halt that steady progress by identifying and dealing with the spiritual issues which are creating the need for the substance.

The damages addictions do to the physical body are massive and are the proper subject of medicine. What is not so well known, however, is the damage done to the more subtle bodies by chemicals—damage to the aura or energy bodies that surround the body, and to the chakras, which are energy exchange points we will study in the next book. Steady abuse of substances like alcohol, sugar, pot, or pills can distort or destroy the energy bodies or aura, the source of our life force energy and cosmic attunement, long before you would be diagnosed as physically addicted.

As yet no one fully understands the physiological or psychological mechanisms of addiction. There seems to be a strong hereditary component to certain addictions. The human brain produces numerous chemicals, called endorphins, which resemble addictive substances on a molecular level. It is possible that some individuals suffer endorphin deficiencies which turn them toward addictive substances as a way of balancing. Others may have more endorphin receptor sites in their brains or more sensitive receptor sites that cannot metabolize substances in the same way non-addicts do. We do not know the exact mechanisms of the process of becoming addicted. We do know, however, that meditation and visualization stimulate the brain to produce endorphins without chemical alterations. Endorphins have a function in the body's immune system and in our general feelings of well-being. So we have found that adding this kind of work to the recovery process has a strong positive effect.

All chemical substances affect the energy body in negative ways to one extent or the other. Alcohol is a heavy poison; from the second week of heavy drinking, you're poisoning the body. Coffee, tea, and sugar affect you, as do excessive amounts of honey. Even drinking too much herb tea or overeating brown rice can harm you. Yet, there are gradations of addictions, with organic substances producing less damage than artificial ones. This is because, in the course of millions of years, the human body has adapted to organic substances but has not had time to learn how to deal with manufactured chemicals.

The Various Paths to Recovery from Addiction

If you're an addict reading this book, you've probably been to therapy, dieted, gone cold turkey, gone to doctors, and probably even been to self-help groups. And it hasn't helped—not for long, anyway. It's not that these things don't work, but what's missing is what this book describes—the work on the spiritual dimension needed to recover completely and to avoid relapse. By spiritual, we refer to the eternal, the cosmic, the greater part of yourself that we as a culture have lost sight of, at the cost of a rising tide of addictions. In our disaffection with churches and organized religion, we've become self-conscious about the word spiritual, and yet spirit simply means life.

In getting free of your addiction, you need health care from physicians, chiropracters, and nutritionists for the body, therapists for the emotions, and self-help groups for support. However, you need to care for the spirit too. This book is a guide for addicts and those who love them—in how to care for the spirit and address the spiritual issues that are a great part of what the addiction is about in the first place.

Together we'll be exploring the spiritual dimensions of addiction, so they can be integrated with the physical and emotional dimensions for a holistic approach. Part of what we'll discover is that addictions have a great deal to do with our culture and its effects on the individual, and with the entire culture's spiritual pathway. We're all one great spirit and we've all been addicts in some of our lifetimes, so the person identifiable as an addict is no more than an exaggeration of the rest of us, performing certain functions for the culture as a whole.

Our Culture as an Addictive One

We're an addictive culture, and your status within it is judged by whether your addiction is viewed as okay or not. If you're a wealth-and-possessions addict, you're a success; if you're a food, alcohol, or drug addict, you're a failure. If you spread your addictions around rather than specializing, so you have more money, more possessions, more sex, more booze, more cocaine, and more food than the rest of us, you're envied. You're a swinger, a person who knows how to live well.

There is much social approval for excess, but not for addiction. Our society abounds in double messages about these substances. Eat hearty but don't get fat. Drink like a man but don't get drunk. Don't feel bad—take something for it, but don't get hooked. The person who is trying to stay away from addiction is often encouraged, cajoled, pressured, and even coerced to take a bite, a drink, a puff. A self-help group is extremely useful in strengthening you against social pressure and in reinforcing your desire to stop.

Addiction is partially due to the dehumanizing effects of our culture. We're masses conforming, not being who we are. For the vast majority of people, work has little value or individuality, little sense of accomplishment. We used to be able to say, for instance, that we built this house that we live in. If everyone who was addicted would drop the addiction overnight, there would be a breakdown in the decaying institutions of this society. Addictions have been used to quiet the unhappy masses since earliest history. For instance, Native Americans and Black slaves were deliberately given liquor to control them and to get them to accept white domination, and these groups still suffer greatly from the heritage of addiction. Marx recognized the use of addiction to control when he said religion was the opiate of the masses. In a time when the masses no longer turn to religion, they simply turn to opium of one kind or another.

Seeking to gain balance on an imbalanced planet is hard and constitutes another pull toward addiction. We're sad at the changes, the waste. We abuse substances to dull the fear of blowing ourselves up, to numb ourselves to the dangers, the crowding. We all feel what's happening to the planet, where we're headed. Addiction is for the purpose of numbing ourselves to knowing, shutting down the feelings. It's a collective choice to, "Eat, drink, and be merry, for tomorrow we may die." It's a reaction, also, to the lack of a sense of planetary purpose and of the sense of oneness we knew when everyone was more attuned to spirit.

We're sad, too, that there's nowhere else on earth to expand to...no frontiers to conquer, no new land. The wish to expand is part of all of us, and lacking somewhere to expand to, we seek to expand by means of more money, more possessions. We have become a consumer focused society, wanting more, more, more. We have to have something going all the time or we feel empty. Emptiness comes from not being in touch with the spiritual side of your being and the other levels of consciousness this book is about.

How Addicts Fit into an Addictive Society

In the evolution of conscious awareness, different groups of people became the metaphoric actors of society's movement in new directions. The blind represent, for the whole, a way of living fully without that metaphor for knowledge that you call light. Simply saying the words "Helen Keller" has made more changes inside people than a hundred thousand hours of radio evangelists. Lesbians and gay men are metaphors for difference—being the same and yet not the same thing. Once the blind were locked away, still the gay are punished.

Addicts of all kinds are metaphors for the different parts of the human species which are struggling to change. When we, as a whole, are less afraid to change, then people will stop drinking, drugs will no longer be taken, and our bodies will not be poisoned anymore. To blame the addict for the addiction is to ignore what's going on in our culture. What you ignore will destroy you. If you pass through fear, you'll be born.

In the same way an individual who's different from the norm can be the target of the family's anxiety and attempts to control, addicts stand in that relationship to society. As we'll see in the chapters about specific substances, addicts have the vision of the changes necessary for all of us to survive and to grow, and they try to channel it. Because society fears the changes inherent in that vision, addicts are singled out and scapegoated.

The Sixties, with visions of social change and experimentation with drugs, showed these principles clearly. We will describe the collective nature of the choice to use drugs to open up certain visions, and the effects of those drugs on the collective evolution, in the later chapters on those particular substances. For some, pot, LSD, and other drugs stimulated the vision of social change. For others, the drug consoled when it became clear that vision wasn't going to manifest overnight. As many people are using chemicals now as in the Sixties, and for many of the same reasons. As a society, following the Sixties, we settled for addiction, because we lacked the courage to change.

If we look at history, addictions increase when cultures are on the brink of opening up to new wisdom. Now, for the first time, we're on the verge of a planetary culture—and, just beyond that, of joining the rest of the universe in off-world travel. The vision of one world is so ancient, and the thought of its imminent realization so splendid, that we're all frightened. People get afraid before a great change, the way a child gets afraid before it loses a baby tooth for the first time. The tooth hurts and itches, and it's too loose, but the child doesn't want to give it up. Neither do we, so we're all busy trying to patch up this old culture that no longer fits.

The Concepts of Power Tools and Light

We'll be using a number of terms and expressions that may not be familiar to you. One we'll return to again and again is power tool. This means anything—whether spiritual practice or chemical substance—which acts on those spiritual realities the way a power mower or electric mixer does in the physical world, to speed up the job at hand. Seeking the power to carry out their purpose, pre-addicts turn to one of the chemical power tools.

The earliest power tools used by people on this planet were natural substances like mushrooms, roots, leaves, and bark. Just as cats understand catnip, many animals understand plants; humans are not alone in this awareness. In fact, humans no longer understand plants in the same way animals do because we've lost our in-touchness with other expressions of life. The earliest chemical process for transmuting chemical substances to release their power was the one that began in the mouth and digestive tract. Smoking, fermentation, and later chemical extraction, and then synthesizing substances all grew out of simple biological processes.

Each chemical power tool will work for a time. But, like a lawn mower gone wild in a cartoon, they will no longer serve us if used too frequently, but will chase us across the grass wildly, trying to devour us. We'll present other tools just as powerful as the chemical tools, if not more so, and without the harmful side effects.

The chief of the power tools we'll be using throughout this book is light—not light from the sun or a light bulb, but inner light. It's the source of visible light, the life force energy, the essence of pure thought, the root of enlightenment. This is the light many psychically gifted people see in auras, those colored energy outlines which surround and radiate from all living things. This light may well be the "visual" effect of the life force or the spirit. These energy outlines have been captured on film in Kirlian photography, so there's proof that they exist. The most interesting of these photographs show a great flash of light from a healer's hands while she is working with someone or even thinking about healing, contrasted with photos of when she is at rest. Light, then, has the power to heal and is involved in the healing process.

Our spoken language reflects a dim perception of this phenomenon in phrases like "to see the light" and "casting a new light on the subject." Exercises given in various chapters will teach you to use this light to heal yourself. We propose it as the substitute and cleanser for the substances you've been using. It's priceless, eternal within us, and only in need of rediscovery.

When we talk about spiritual here, we usually mean Subtle, that is, those aspects of reality we don't perceive with the five senses, as in the subtle or energy body. So when we talk about light, it's not just a metaphor for a mental process, but a drawing into ourselves of ever present subtle or spiritual essence. Matter is only dense spirit. Matter gets more and more refined—to liquid, gas, or energy.

You don't need a religious form—a church or temple—to have a spiritual content, any more than religion or national law can govern matter's transformation into its various levels of density. Beginning to be more conscious of these levels and learning to manipulate them in a conscious, positive fashion rather than by using an addictive substance to manipulate them is a key to your healing.

Some of you are already familiar with this kind of work, either through training or through a natural sensitivity to it, but for others it may be new. Do not be dismayed if you cannot see this light. Many of the addicts who worked with us and were helped by this material never saw it and nonetheless experienced its healing effects. The blind do not have to see sunshine to feel its loving touch on their skin. Each of us perceives it in our own way. Some feel it as movement, others as a great warmth or gentle tingling. So trust yourself. Your spiritual self will create the light just as ingeniously as it created your body and consciousness. As you work with these techniques, you'll find the effects growing stronger, just as a runner increases in stamina by running.

EXERCISE: Building a Bubble of White Light and Contacting Your Core Self

Many of the exercises and processes in this book start with a bubble of light, often white, but sometimes in other colors. A bubble of white light is also a safe place for many of the turmoils of recovery, so it's a basic healing tool. The following exercise will help you to create it.

1. Sit quietly in a comfortable place, on a pillow, in a soft chair, on your bed, with your eyes closed. Some of you may prefer to sit in lotus position, others may prefer to have your feet on the floor. Be aware of your body as you sit. Notice places that are tense, twitchy, or painful.

2. Become aware of your breathing. Feel the movement of inhalation and exhalation, as it rises and falls in your body. Feel this movement starting in your abdomen. If you have trouble feeling it there, you may want to take several deep breaths and force your abdomen out to inhale and pull it in to exhale, so your mind and body get the sense of this movement. Then slowly let your body do this on its own. Notice the changes in your spine also. Feel how it undulates each time you inhale and exhale.

3. Feel that, as you do this, you open up your consciousness to the ultimate, eternal, creative part of yourself. This is the part we call the Core Self and others call the soul or higher self. Know that you have the power to evoke this part of yourself simply by calling its name, much as those who pray evoke the Divine by calling on it. Know that your Core Self is a spark of the Divine. Remember that no matter how distant from it you might feel in certain parts of your life, there is, in truth, a strong connection between you, your Core Self, and the Divine.

4. Feel that you can breathe into any parts of your body which are tense or uncomfortable. Draw the energy of each breath into those areas as you inhale, and feel that each time you exhale, you're releasing a bit more of the stress, tension, or pain that is there. As you do this, your body will relax, soften, and open.

5. As distracting thoughts rise up, look at them, feel them, but stay connected with your breathing. Go back to being aware of the inflow and outflow of breath if you find yourself going off with your thoughts. Honor those thoughts, hold them, but do not focus on them now.

6. Slowly begin to feel that energy is flowing around you, that light is swirling around you. A bird once had its shell, we ourselves once floated in the safety of our placental egg, in the bodies of our mothers. Some part of your consciousness knows and remembers this feeling of being contained and protected. Feel that out of the light a bubble, an egg, begins to form around you. It contains your entire body. It has thickness and solidness and begins to glow more and more brightly, as pure white, clear light, as you conjure it up around you.

7. Sit quietly in this egg, this bubble. Continue to feel your breath. Some may not be able to get this sense of a bubble the first time. Each time you come back to do this exercise, you'll be strengthening the bubble, strengthening your visualizing muscles.

Be aware of any changes that may happen in your body and in the way you feel when you sit in the bubble. Create it around you whenever you're tired, afraid, or feel yourself craving something. Each time you do this, you strengthen the bubble, making it more real. You're consciously working with the subtle energy around you to help you, to heal you, to serve you better. Eventually, you'll be able to create the bubble around you in an instant. Eventually, it will be as perceptible around you as your clothing and just as real.

The Vision of the Life Task and Addiction

We are fourfold beings—mind, emotions, body, and spirit. Our sense of vision is one of the major attributes of our minds. We create our life vision when we are on the spiritual plane, both before birth and during our earthly lives, in dreams and altered states of consciousness such as those induced by drugs. In the course of our lives, however, it's easy to become disconnected from that vision. The vision or dream is always bigger than the actuality. We need the picture to be that big in order to gather energy to move it from the astral to the psychic plane...like how big things are when projected on a movie screen, and how stirring.

Addiction can begin with the use of any substance to help you get back the vision of your life tasks or purposes and to have the strength to tackle them. Once addicts recognize that what becomes hideously self-destructive in the end once began as a positive impulse, it will be easier to get back to positive movement. It is important to break the modern belief that everything we do is self-destructive.

At the start, the addictive substance—sugar, alcohol, drugs, whatever—may have been used because of unconscious knowledge that such substances are tools of power, inducing strength and dampening fear. This knowledge is reflected by the slang term "Dutch courage" for a drink taken to give you the nerve to do something difficult, like ask for a raise. If you need Dutch courage several times a day, that's addiction.

The process of addiction is often as follows: some people are overwhelmed by their vision of life and feel inadequate. They begin to use the drug as a tool of power, hoping it will give them strength to manifest the whole vision. This may work at first, but once the power tool is habitually misused, it starts to destroy the energy body, further handicapping the person. The hope of manifestation goes down the drain. These people are stuck with the power tool, which has now gained power over them and will eventually damage the physical body too.

The addict, seeing the vision in its larger dimensions, doesn't realize the manifestation can never be as grand as the vision, but energy and strength can be drawn from its grandness. This larger-than-life vision both awes and overwhelms in its splendor. People who become addicts are often fearful of trying to measure up to what they see, getting discouraged when their efforts aren't the same as the vision. This inability to accept one's visions is often due to the addicts' childhood environment and the lack of support for their uniqueness. Many have addicted parents, come from dysfunctional families or chronically depressed ones, where what is good is undervalued, what is true is not perceived clearly, and what is possible is misunderstood. The addictive substance then becomes a tool to dull both the vision and the unhappiness at not fulfilling it.

The concept of vision as we use it here is not meant to be taken literally. A visionary is a dreamer, and most addicts are visionaries at heart. But your visions may not be something you see with your eyes. If you are a songwriter, you probably don't see the songs—you hear them. If you are a potter, you may not see the shapes—you feel them. If you are a dancer, you don't always see the dance—you feel it moving within you. Each of you will use your visions in a way that is unique and appropriate to yourself, but you have the full and rich capacity to use them to help yourself. In fact, since running from the vision contributed to your addiction, getting back to your vision and finding out how to use it are essential to healing yourself of the addiction and its destructive effects on your life. No doubt you ran because it looked so big and so impossible. How could you do it alone? You don't have to do it alone. None of us do.

Those who become addicts are often psychic, creative, visionary people. In the before-birth period of selecting the life task, they may have made the choice to do something difficult. It is like flowers—some choose to grow in the field, where growth is easy, and some choose to grow up through cracks in the sidewalk, where it is very hard going. Addicts are often the flowers that grow up through the cracks, choosing a difficult, challenging childhood to test and refine their strength, but sometimes getting overwhelmed by the test.

In that sense, addicts are often courageous, even though we like to think of them as weak. A Bowery Bum needs far more strength and courage to stay alive, to continue to struggle, than the man on Easy Street. Addicts are often doubly courageous, in that despite the handicap of a debilitated energy body due to the drug, many still do achieve wonderful things. You need only think of the great writers, artists, and political figures who were addicted, yet still did remarkable things. Even ordinary addicts are courageous because, despite fear of their task or disappointment in the manifestation, they did not choose suicide. There is further courage in the fact that the addict keeps on struggling to keep the vision alive in a world that denies the validity of vision. Addicts need to feel a sense of their own strength.

In the addicted person, you often hear the dream, "...when I write my great novel," "...when I'm discovered and perform in Madison Square Garden," "...when I get the bugs out of this invention." These grandiose notions are often ridiculed as "pipe dreams," but the phenomenon is evidence of the tendency for the vision to be much larger than the manifestation. It's a major indictment of our society that it contributes in so many ways to the problem of addictions. Society doesn't honor visions or dreams, only manifestations. It also reinforces the addict's grandiosity, because it doesn't value small successes or small efforts, only big ones.

Addicts are deeply disappointed when the manifestation is small, so that even a success in the world's terms may not satisfy them, and they use their substance to dull the disappointment. A critical point in the addictive process often comes either with a vision that fails or success that doesn't measure up to expectations, from a failed career to a failed love affair.

The tendency to be afraid of the task and feel inadequate to fulfill it is particularly strong when a young person, aware of the task or addicted to a particular vision at a very young age, doesn't see that there are many possible visions. A six-year-old, aware of the life purpose to write a particular novel, can easily become overwhelmed. At six you can barely write a sentence, so it's hard to feel capable of a novel. The child who knows too much sets up the seeds of addiction. Even though the child's capabilities change, the sense of inadequacy, unconsciously held, may remain.

Our society further contributes to the problem by believing that children are a different species of human than adults, and that children's visions are not to be listened to. Thus, there's terror in children who have a vision, a terror of how they are going to make this species change from child to adult. We are a society where children are guardians of the visions, but only adults are capable of manifestation.

The young successful person may also have a problem. How many young stars wind up dying of drugs? People who are successful at a young age may have only come to do one particular thing, something society needs at that exact moment in time for its further development. When the task is done, they may lack a sense of purpose or may fear they cannot find a new vision. Conceivably, one could achieve something important by age 25 and spend the rest of that life with no major problems and no heavy responsibilities. Yet in our society, the demand is always for more, more, more. If you achieve one thing, the pressure is on to achieve something even bigger. Society doesn't allow you to coast, or it calls you a has-been. Successful young people may turn to addiction as a way of dealing with the achievement orientation of our society and the pressure put upon them if they have succeeded.

Another case in point is the person we'd call a visionary, someone whose life task is related to some future need or condition in our society. Karmically, such a person has come to plant the seeds of others' visions or to take the action that makes a later development possible. This could be in broader social terms—the scientist or artist who is years ahead of our time and whose ideas are put into practice much later.   Or, it may be in more personal terms—the person whose major purpose is to be the parent of someone who makes an important contribution, whether or not it's a notable one. At some level, the forerunner may know the whole vision of the future and be frustrated at not being able to manifest it in the here and now, turning to the addiction to deal with the pain. It's difficult, and lonely too, to be ahead of your time, thus the visionary may use a substance to escape that loneliness.

For the person whose addiction is an attempt to hide from the vision, no real healing of the addiction can come without an awareness of the vision as well. That is, you need to find out what life task you created for yourself in that before-birth period and get to work on it. But don't think you must have one single, stirring life task to accomplish. We all have numerous tasks or purposes, possibly within the context of a life path or life work. Not everyone was born to walk on the moon, most of us have life tasks that will never make the newspapers, but all of us are here to contribute something to the world we live in. What you are looking for, then, is to find what you came here to contribute. An important exercise to help you get back in touch with that contribution would be to make a list of everything you've ever thought of doing, even the silliest.   Pay particular attention to those "childish" visions you had at seven or so ("When I grow up I'm going to..."). They may not be so far-fetched, reduced from astral vision size down to manifestation size. Exercises in Chapter Two will further help you identify and heal your vision.

Anima, Animus and Addiction

We've all lived lives as both sexes, and all contain within us an aspect of the sex we've chosen not to manifest physically in our present lives. The female aspect of a man has been called his anima, while the male aspect of a woman has been called her animus. Because we live in a culture with very narrow views of gender roles, we've all tried to repress our contra-sexual aspects. Part of our healing on a global level is an awakening into consciousness of our wholeness, of our androgynous natures. Often, however, this repression is of particular importance to recovering addicts. It may be the male aspect of a woman or the female aspect of a man that carries much of the "charge," the pattern for the addiction.   If the addiction occurred, because you denied this part of yourself, it may very well seem that it comes from somewhere else and isn't part of you at all.

If this is the case, it may be frightening to start to get in touch with these parts of yourself because of cultural repression.   In many cases, it may have been fear of your anima or animus that caused you to drink or do drugs in the first place. We're taught to be manly men and womanly women, and contra-sexual aspects are considered inappropriate to express. Much of this has to do with the age-old conflicts between the sexes that began in the matriarchy and continued, but in a different fashion, in the patriarchy.   Androgynous, gay, and bisexual people have suffered for generations from society's hatred and fear of anyone who steps out of the approved gender roles, however these roles might change in different times and places. But we're reaching the point in our history where a major part of our individual and collective work is about accepting and balancing out these two energies.

There are several ways to start on this work. You might begin by just thinking about and accepting those parts of you that are not considered gender-appropriate. If the thought of doing this immediately makes you want to refuse, you probably need to do it. Another way to do it is to sit in your bubble and begin to experience yourself as the opposite sex from the one you are now. Try to see yourself and feel as clearly as possible. Try to get a sense of what you think and feel and do in the world.

If your parents are alive or there's someone else you can ask, find out what you would have been named if you had been born the other sex. This is empowering to the animus and anima. We know ourselves by our names. If you cannot find out this information, name your anima or animus yourself. Then try to respond to that name with the same fullness you do when you are called by your given name.

When the sense of your contra-sexual side has grown strong, it may be time to sit in your bubble and talk to it or let it talk to you. Ask it about your patterns of addiction. Let that information surface and explore it. You may find that it's the source of a great deal of information and insight that the outer you did not have access to.

Some of the patterns of addiction come from our experiences as members of the opposite sex in our past lives. When you get to the chapter on the karma of addiction you may want to do the exercises described there to get in touch with past lives so that you can ask this question of them.

Dr.C.G. Jung was the pioneer in working with the anima and the animus. You might consider doing Jungian therapy for a while if this work seems important but difficult for you to do on your own. Gestalt therapy will also approach this problem, but from a different direction, as will polarity therapy, balancing you on a more physical level. Rebirthing work can help to clear out parental reactions to your gender when you were born and to your contra-sexual side.

When you do the exercise in the book for getting in touch with your spiritual friends, if they always appear as the same sex you are now, make a conscious effort to reach out to companions of the other gender. This will be a source of nurturing, strength, and acceptance on that plane that will ripple out into your day-to-day life.

Working with Your Shadow

There's another important concept that Jung explored, and that's what he called the shadow. The shadow is the internal, psychospiritual repository of everything about ourselves we wish to deny. It's all that our families, our society, and we ourselves consider bad, evil, and shameful. Most often these are considered negative traits. Because we were so severely punished for temper tantrums, we learn to control them by shunting our anger into our shadows, so that it looks like we outgrew it or finally learned to deal with it. We spend the rest of our lives as dishrags—but we don't get angry anymore. Sometimes, however, these are more positive traits that we push away. Often a creative child in a noncreative family, or a psychic child, is teased and tormented for the gift until that too gets buried deep down in the shadow.

If things stayed in the shadow, that might be okay. But they don't. We have to deal with them at some point in our lives. If we don't, we'll continue to work at being good, but we'll never become whole. Addictive behavior is often caused by the need to keep traits hidden in our shadows. We use them as tools to push down that which is considered unacceptable. But just as often, addiction provides the doorway through which the shadow escapes. The loving husband and father next door gets drunk and turns into the monster he's been repressing for twenty years. The overburdened homemaker across the hall smokes a few joints and goes home with the hot teenager from the other side of town.

We all want to be good, kind, and nice, but inside all of us is a monster we pretend is not there. Addiction can and usually will release it. How much crime and violence accompany addiction? How much abuse, murder, and destruction of property, families, and lives can occur? Very often it's the destructive shadow elements that lead one into addiction, as self-punishment and family punishment. If the shadow is repressed for too long, it will begin to scream out for attention. And if that attention is not given, the ego may lead one down the path of addiction in order to release the shadow.

It's a difficult path toward wholeness, and a painful one. How many people you know have not survived it? How close have you come to not surviving it, in order to meet face-to-face all the hidden, ugly parts of who you are? We cannot sweep them under the rug. They do not go away.

The only way we can change them is to face them and to see that very often that which has festered and turned bad is only a wound in the child part of ourselves in need of the comfort and understanding. Many of the tools we suggested in the section above will be of use to you in this problem.

But if it was frightening to accept the opposite sex part of you, it may be even harder to accept the bad side of you. You don't have to do this work alone. Remember that.

A tool to work with on your own, however, is to sit in your bubble and visualize a large dark screen just outside of it. This screen is your shadow projected outwards. Many addicts project their shadows onto someone else or onto society. This is you and your shadow. And as you breathe deeply and feel strong, you can begin to see the images of yourself that you have repressed, and that you need to incorporate into your psyche in order to become whole. Nothing can show up here that is not a part of your life and your history. Often we're afraid that if we see our shadows, it will be a demon or a devil staring back at us. But in truth, the shadow's always just a hurt and needy child, not a Hitler, but a being hungry for love and attention. So after the images come up, you may need to take the child you were in your lap and hold it for a while.

Death, Mediumship, and Addiction

Anyone who has been an addict has danced the fine line between life and death, perhaps with an immediacy far stronger than that of other people. There's still a romanticism attached to those who died of their addictions. We make them cult figures. But it's time to release that attitude.

There was a time in our history when the boundaries between life and death were not so clear-cut. People were not so afraid of dying as we are now because they were accustomed to wandering out into nonphysical dimensions of reality. They were also accustomed to experiences and rituals where there was clear communication with those who had died. For us today, however, life is one thing and death is another. They are separate in our minds, not interwoven.

But many of us sense that this is not the way things really are. Many of us have been shamans and spirit-talkers in other lives. We remember this on some deep level. Often people turn to addictive substances in fear of opening up to this level of awareness, just as others turn to them in the hopes of breaking through to it. And some of you may be bouncing back and forth between these two positions.

Often the death of a loved one, especially when we are young, is a hidden causal factor in addiction. On occasion, a loved one who has died may try to communicate with someone who is living. Addiction may be used to block out of consciousness what the heart may hunger for consciously.

Death is a vast unknown domain to explore, but we don't need to use our addictions as telescopes. When we are far from our Core Selves, dying may appear as a healing, as a total amputation of a gangrenous life. But as we master the tools of consciousness altering, we will understand our immortality, in and out of our bodies. We'll be able to communicate again with other immortals, and then we can use each chosen physical life fully and joyfully.

We create our deaths as much as we create our lives. You may find it helpful to visualize yourself as a wise old being getting ready to depart this current life. Talk to yourself as you will be then. Let that self teach you things you have not been able to see yet. Life changes—but it does not stop. It is time for us to remember that.

Energy and How It Applies to Addiction

Another concept we'll be using frequently is that of energy. For instance, we'll refer to the energy body, which coexists with the physical body and is made up of light and of life force energy. Since spiritual ideas are becoming somewhat popularized, people do speak of energy now. For instance, someone might say, "The energy in this room is intense," or "I really like your energy."

Basically, we're referring to the life force energy, the charge of vitality which comes from spirit and which sustains our lives. The energy we get from food is not what keeps us alive, because dying people eat and yet the life force ebbs away. We're all fed this energy continuously from our Core Selves, and we can draw on it more consciously, as we'll learn to do in this book. Yet the addicted person, and increasingly all of us, will seek it in an external source, such as a chemical, another person, or electronic stimulation.

One of the seeds of addiction is that as much as we seek energy, we also fear it and want to control it. This fear is not very different from the fear little children have when they need to go to the bathroom late at night. But what about the fear that attends the abilities no one ever speaks of? What about the fear of seeing the future, or the fear of hearing the aura of a sick friend or relative? What about the fear of listening to long dead people. Nobody speaks of this at all, so the fear is stronger.

The fear will be greater when one is afraid of a part of the self that no one speaks about, the Core Self and the vision of those greater realities. If they do speak about it, they use words like "Out Of Touch" or "Dreamer" or "Crazy." The need to hide from it will be stronger. The energy is there, however, unseen or unknown, and it will come out, no matter how we try to block it. We may turn to an addictive substance in order to drown it or lose it in clouds of smoke. However, it will always come back, all the more strongly for having been repressed. Similarly, when a dam explodes, it destroys with that which is only a billion cups of tea or a million morning showers. Each cup is harmless alone, each is healing alone.

As we'll see more clearly in the chapters on various addictions in the next book, the addict turns to the power tool for more energy to manifest the life tasks or visions. At first it works, but it winds up leeching the energy and destroying the vision. The exercise which follows is one for perceiving the effect of the substances you abuse on your energy body. (If you are the loved one of an addict, you might want to use it to test your loved one's effect on you, or the effects of one of your own addictions, like television or coffee.)

EXERCISE: Seeing the Effect of Addiction on the Energy Body.

1. Sit quietly, breathe, deeply, and imagine that you're sitting in your bubble of white light.

2. Visualize the substance that you're addicted to on the outside of your bubble. Picture the drink, a cigarette, a joint, a brownie, a couple of pills, or whatever.

3. Slowly bring the substance closer and closer to the outside of the bubble. Notice what happens to the bubble as you bring it nearer. Notice what happens to the light. Does it remain as strong, does the light fade, or does the bubble change?

4. Now move the substance away from the bubble and notice how the bubble changes. Try this for a while, bringing the substance toward and away from your energy field, and notice the changes. You've created a safe and healing space within the bubble. What happens to it when you bring this substance near to it? Do certain parts of your body change, or do certain areas of the bubble change? (You may wish to write those changes down and refer to them as you read the chapter on the energy body.)

5. Release the substance. Dissolve it in your mind. Now just feel and see your bubble around you. How is it different without the substance nearby. How has it changed?

How Chemical Pollution Adds to the Growth of Addiction

As suggested earlier, the human body has been exposed to organic substances for millions of years and is composed of similar substances. But this is not so with artificial chemicals. We're all continuously exposed to plastics, cosmetics, food additives, air pollutants, synthetic clothing, and pharmaceutical products, which harm the energy body. (If you think this is not so, try the above exercise on your diet cola, hair dye, or birth control pills.) This exposure begins before birth, through our mothers' bodies. So many of us were born with pain killers circulating through us, numbing us just when we were ready to slip out into the light, predisposing us toward chemical substance abuse later in our lives.

There's an inequity in the distribution of the damage, in that working-class people are far more likely to be exposed to industrial chemicals on the job. This poisoning of the subtle bodies leads to dissatisfaction and anger, which can be vented in hostile and aggressive acts. Affluent people look down their noses at this kind of aggression, attributing it to "lower class" behavior, or even to racial behavior, since poverty clings to the minorities in our land. They don't see it as a result of chemical poisoning created by their addictive demands for more and more products or services. Since we senselessly waste things, the demand for such products is endless. People who work in settings where there's this kind of pollution may need to do the exercises on cleansing the energy body, given in the next book, regularly to prevent damage and ease the pull to addiction.

Another modern invention which affects the energy field of practically everybody in our nation is television. Television is light that constantly moves and changes, penetrating your energy bodies and creating little holes. Television addicts are a national phenomenon too, and such people may even go into withdrawal when they stop abruptly. Television addicts are often people whose vision is locked deep inside. They subliminally recognize the light and know that it is penetrating their energy field. They think the penetration will inspire their own vision, but instead it robs them of vision and of the time to fulfill it. They are left needing the constant nourishment of the canned visions on television. Watching also limits our interaction with others and contributes to the love starvation that is so widespread. This holds true for video games and computer terminals when used to excess.

The Special Spiritual Power of Working with a Group

In line with what we have been saying about energy, work with a group can be a potent factor in your healing. Although addicts often become isolated and afraid of others, you should not tackle your recovery single-handedly. The united energy field of a group is always more powerful than that of an individual working alone. There are also spiritual beings and helpers on other planes who work with such groups, enhancing their healing energy. Thus, you may find it useful to work through the exercises in this book with your family and friends. Also remember to invite your own guides, known or unknown, in to work with you.

Another reason a group is powerful is that, even though you may think your addiction is a private matter, it's not entirely so. The wish to drink, take drugs, or eat is strengthened by the intentions, vibrations, and desires of the people who produce and sell the products. Our culture depends on alcohol and other drugs, so you also have to overcome the effects of programming, social pressure, and advertising. For all these reasons, a group has more power to withstand the urge to relapse than you have alone.

There are, for instance, Twelve-Step anonymous programs similar to A.A. for every addiction you can imagine and some you haven't heard of. There are over 150 of such programs, including Emotions Anonymous, Gamblers Anonymous, Overeaters Anonymous, and Debtors Anonymous. Your public library should have a directory of local or national self-help programs and possibly even the manuals they use. If you're the loved one of an addict, there are groups for you too, as you shouldn't have to withstand the pain and confusion alone.

The Healing Crisis

Filthy water traveling through a tube will deposit debris

along the course of the tube, yet the water will keep trying to force itself through until the tube is so encrusted that the water backs up and something bursts. You don't have to let it go that far; you can purify the water by cleansing the accumulated wastes. You can purify the water itself until it's perfect, but if the debris remains in the tube, it's going to repollute it. When you start dredging, however, the healing crisis begins. The encrusted garbage begins to surface, and the pure waters you've worked so hard for are infected. If you don't know this is going to happen, you can drown in the deep despair of saying, "See, I did all the best things possible for myself, and even they didn't work." STOP, if you hear yourself say that, and know the healing crisis has begun. You're cleaning out the accumulated debris—the fear, the failure, the anger, the resentment—and for a while it's going to stink like crazy.

It's best to have a friend who knows what you're going through—to hug you and hold you and say, "This, too, will pass." For those of you who haven't such a friend, be that friend to yourself and let this book be your friend. Never let yourself forget that however much these difficulties resemble the difficulties of the past, they are only the accumulated debris of the past being released. You're not going backwards. Reach out to your guides, known or unknown, when you get to this place—and know that you're not alone. (An exercise later in this chapter will show you how to do this, if you aren't already aware of any guides.)

This healing crisis follows your conscious decision to change and to cleanse yourself. Many who have started on this path have been plunged into further despair through not understanding what was happening. This may have happened to you often in your past as you tried to let go of the addiction. Do not despair. This period will not be easy, but if you trust the cleansing and if you keep on cleansing, it will pass.

If the addiction has been to keep feelings down, you have to expect them to re-emerge bit by bit when you stop. Just as you detoxify on the physical level, you can expect detoxification on the emotional level as well. The important thing is not to let any of the feelings overwhelm you or to get too attached to them. They pass, just as the symptoms of physical detoxification pass. They can tell you a great deal about yourself and the conflicts you've been hiding from, but they're likely to be exaggerated from being pent up so long.

Feelings may come up from your past—anger, resentment, hurt—and you may try to attach them to something in the present. ("It's not logical," you say to yourself, "to be so angry about something that happened twenty years ago.") For instance, you may suddenly be furious at a lover who left you ten years ago, but you inappropriately direct that anger toward your present lover, a family member, or a good friend. You may attribute it to something this person has just done, so you can say you have cause for the anger...but not to that extreme. Be aware of this tendency to displace feelings and keep redirecting them to the proper target.

Also, don't try to rationalize the feelings away. ("That's all in the past. It doesn't make sense to cry over it.") Don't cover them over with phony forgiveness or sweetness and light. Real forgiveness and acceptance will come later, as you work the exercises through to completion, but not until you've allowed yourself to experience the rage or hurt fully.

Eating sugar, drinking, smoking too much, or using drugs will shut the process off or dull its impact, so stay away from them. If you allow the feelings to come up and neither act on them impulsively nor do anything to shut them down, you get through them much faster and you have a better opportunity to heal than when you repress them. We never give ourselves more than we can handle. And we never begin this process until we are strong enough to handle it, even though we may feel very weak while we're going through it.

It helps, however, to know that it passes, that it relates to the work you are doing on yourself, and that it is healing in and of itself. The healing crisis is like a fever that spikes before getting better, like the good cry that makes you feel better, or like the big fight that clears the air in a relationship. If you let it happen and don't hold back, you will get relief. It is like vomiting. When your stomach is upset and you need to get rid of what you ate, you feel nauseated. The process of vomiting is awful, but when you've removed all that poisonous garbage from your system, your stomach settles down, and you feel better. When unpleasant feelings start to come up, just tell yourself that you're vomiting and you're going to feel better when you get all that garbage out. It's like being in the middle of cleaning your house and thinking it's more of a mess than when you started.

There are, however, things you can do to transmute the feelings as they come up. You can put a bubble of white light around yourself, as you learned to do earlier in this chapter.   As the feelings surge, blaze the light up brighter and know that the feelings are being consumed and transformed by it. You are letting go of the pain of the experience but you are being enlightened by it—the light helps you learn from the experience so that you need not repeat your mistakes. The exercise below will also help you get through the tough times, by creating a safe space.

EXERCISE: Creating A Safe Space and Connecting with Your Spiritual Friends

After you are comfortable with creating your bubble, you may want to use it in other ways. It's easy to feel isolated from the world when you're addicted, and it's easy to feel unsafe in the world too. The following exercise is a tool for helping you feel safe again, by creating a safe place to carry inside that you can tap into anywhere, any time of day, at work, at home, on a bus, waiting in line at the bank, or waiting for a job interview.

1. Sit quietly, feel your breath, and create your bubble around you.

2. This time, when the bubble is very clear to you, feel that each time you inhale and exhale, your bubble is expanding, like a balloon.

3. Think of the most beautiful place you have ever been, or create in your mind the image of the perfect room, the

perfect place. Is it a beach, a crystal tower, or a castle? Create all the details of your own perfect place as clearly as possible, so that your bubble contains it all.

4. Whenever you are feeling tired, frightened, or alone, know that you can come back to this place and feel recharged and healed by it. It is your own safe and perfect place. Although it is not physically real, it is real in your consciousness. When you find yourself slipping into negativity and hear running through your mindall your old stories of blame, guilt, shame, or anger, come to this safe place.

5. Go back to your bubble again, and create your safe place around you. Feel that somewhere in your space a small, soft light begins to flicker and glow. Slowly this light begins to grow and grow. This light is the presence of your guide, your spiritual friend, beginning to manifest consciously. It may remain just a light, or it may solidify into a plant, an animal, a person, or even an angel. Feel your friend reach out to you, reach out with love and support, with comfort and strength. Know that you are not alone.

Know that whenever you reach out for this light, your friend will be there. You'll find different friends at different times in your recovery and for different needs. When you're feeling alone, frightened, in need of power and understanding, know that a spiritual friend will be there too. Like any friendship, the more you reach out, the more time you spend together, the deeper and clearer your bond will become.

Guidelines for the Healing Work

If you go at healing yourself as compulsively as you went at your addiction, you can mess yourself up. For that reason, certain guidelines have evolved as safeguards. They are needed to combat that urge to excess which always said, "If two drinks are good, five are better." You need resting spaces in the work, to let the healing complete itself and to disperse the accumulations of toxins which the exercises bring to the surface. Otherwise, you can build up an energy body overload and short-circuit yourself.

1. Never work on the exercises more than five days in a row. Then rest for two days. It's all right to sit in your bubble to meditate for a short time each day.

2. Take on only one major exercise or project in a week, let's say the cleansing of fear or anger or the physical cleansing. Even if you finish in less than five days, or if you try it and decide you aren't ready for that particular project, just stop for the week.

3. Work with at least one other person if at all possible.

4. Always put yourself in a bubble and call on your Core Self before beginning.

5. If you're working on the exercises regularly, and you start feeling harassed, pushed, stressed, or adrift, take a vacation from the exercises for a week or more. You may need some time to clear out the overload.

6. Don't neglect your health care, therapy, or self-help group, as all these things contribute to different facets of recovery from addictions. Don't try to do it alone.

7. Lead a well-balanced life in terms of sleep, exercise, and nutrition, as deficits in these three areas can produce needless physical and emotional stress. The anonymous programs use the slogan H.A.L.T. as a warning; that is, never get too Hungry, Angry, Lonely, or Tired, or you're more vulnerable to relapse.

Whenever drink, drug, or food signals become strong, stop the project you are working on and go back to basic white light, calling on your Core Self for help. When the signals subside and you have rested sufficiently, your project for next week should be to go back one, two, or three exercises, because you may very well have incompletely processed those experiences.

It might be useful to keep a log of which exercises you've gone through and your responses to them, so you can look back on your path later, or know where to go if you need to backtrack for a while. You may also find it useful to tape record each of the exercises, going through each step slowly, with long pauses between steps. This way you can hear them in your own voice as you work through them, and you won't have to keep opening your eyes and picking up the book.

You may wonder whether you need to go through this book, doing all the exercises in order. Trust your own inner wisdom. You will be more drawn to certain exercises and certain sections than to others, and those are the ones you should turn to. Each person is different, the course of each addiction is different, and so is the recovery. This book is like a giant tool chest, with tools for many different uses. But you are the carpenter, the mechanic, the engineer who knows the best time and the best use of each of these tools. Use them in good health.

The Healing Process

The amount of time the healing takes varies greatly with the individual, but don't think you can accomplish it in a week.   In more severe cases, it may take two or three months of constant work to get through the healing crisis itself, and more time than that for the total healing. You may emerge at the end of this weakened and somewhat depressed, but you will be cleansed and ready to begin making changes. The tube will be clear, and if you keep on pumping clear water through it, you will surely be living in health.

Part of the process in the beginning is creating the bubble of white light and feeling safe and comfortable in it. You should do that first as long as you need to—even if it takes a few days—before beginning any of the other exercises.

Anytime you feel resistance arising to the work, you should stop what you're doing and just go back to the bubble.

You cannot always be doing something. There are cycles of activity and rest. Sometimes what we might call resistance merely shows we've come to the end of one cycle and we shouldn't be pushing ourselves to do something. Addictive people are prone to keep on pushing themselves, demanding more. Sometimes when you feel resistance, you should stop and return to a resting place just to give yourself time to be, to find peace in the sphere of light, to let the healing be completed on all levels. Then go back and try something else. Rest can change the nature of resentment, because we can resent having to change. We need a space in which to feel all right about being the way we are. Thus, we can rest to change resistance, without having to consciously understand why we resist.

After all, we all have our own unique body, emotional makeup, and history—both in this life and in relevant past lives. Since we are all as unique as our fingerprints, the exercises you do, the order in which you do them, and the number of times you do them will also be unique. The need and the recovery of each individual who uses this book will be different. However, we will offer some general guidelines a bit later. The main thing is to be as patient and tender with yourself as you would with someone who has been ill. Your vitality will come back on a physical level long before your emotional and spiritual vitality are restored. Thus you may be puzzled and impatient when these subtler levels seem to take so long. Don't push yourself, don't judge your progress. You may have been an addict for many lifetimes. Do you expect to get through all that in a month? Just know that you cannot do it all at once—cannot speed-read your way through this book, cannot fast-forward through the healing.

Some exercises will be easier for you than others. Pay particular attention to the ones you have difficulty with, as those are generally areas where you need lots of work. Do it at your own pace. If the anger part is difficult, for instance, take your time with it. It might take you a week to feel the anger, another week to project it. It's not so simple as the steps of the written exercise. Do it a bit at a time and also work on something else that's easier for you. You will also find yourself doing certain things over and over at different periods of your recovery—getting at deeper and deeper levels of the same problem, the same experience, the same feeling. That's fine. It takes what it takes.

There's also another kind of crisis when you get through—a crisis of wellness. You're healthier now and you don't know what to do with it. It's like going to a foreign country you've always wanted to visit, but once you arrive you need a map and a guide. And because some people chose their addiction to keep from going on with their lives, good health can suddenly become quite fearsome. If that fear arises, go back to the exercise on creating a safe space.

1 *The American Heritage Dictionary of the English Language*, (N.Y: Houghton Mifflin, 1982).

CHAPTER TWO

USING THE POWER OF THE MIND TO TRANSFORM YOUR ADDICTION AND OTHER NEGATIVE THOUGHT PATTERNS

Addicts are so used to thinking of the mind as the thing that leads them into trouble, as the source of the voice that says, "Drink this, smoke this, eat this." It seems like the source of constant, endless, pointless inner chatter. Because of this, many addicts have distanced themselves from the positive aspects, the healing aspects, of the power of the mind. When used rightly, the mind is one of our greatest healers.

We want here to stimulate the positive, life-supporting muscles of consciousness. Initially, this work will balance out the negative ways you use your mind. But in time, as you work through this book, you'll find you have done a spring cleaning of the brain, thrown out old self-defeating patterns originating in negative thoughts, and started to fill your mental house with all sorts of beautiful new mental possessions.

So much of what you experience in the world is what you create in your thoughts and therefore attract into your lives. Most of this process is unconscious and goes back to thought patterns created in childhood. They may or may not have worked to preserve and protect you then, but they probably do not support the way you are trying to live in the world as an adult. The study of metaphysics is about changing thought patterns, but this isn't really a chapter about metaphysics in general. Instead it's a practical guide for addicts in changing their thought patterns. Books on metaphysics are listed in the bibliography in the Appendix, for those who want to go further. Most especially, we would recommend the Seth books, by Jane Roberts.

The New Power Tools We'll Use in This Book

Throughout this book we use the term "power tool" to refer to anything that aids us in making use of our innate spiritual power in the world. We include addictive substances among our list of power tools, for they've been used for thousand of years to gain vision and insight. But the dangers of these tools are obvious to everyone. And as human beings on this planet evolve, the use of these particular power tools will decrease and eventually disappear.

The function of a power tool is to alter your brain waves, your regular patterns of consciousness, so you can channel your thoughts through different frequencies of energy and information. As you well know, chemical power tools don't do the job effectively, because of their side effects. There are other tools that do the same job with no side effects, no damage to the physical body, your thought patterns, or your emotions. There are many power methodologies used by healers, such as acupuncture, herbs, and reiki. However, the three which Andrew and Donna have used effectively in their work with recovering addicts and others who need healing are light, crystals, and essences.

Flower and gem essences, which we'll learn about in Chapters Three and Four, are power tools of the future which are becoming more and more well known right now. Crystals, the subject of Chapter Four, have been used by healers for thousands of years. They are being introduced to mass culture at this time and are being used in new ways that will help carry us into the future. Visualization tools are ancient too, but they're taking on new form and depth in this time. So while we still refer to sugar, alcohol, and other drugs as power tools, it's our intention to present you with a wide array of alternate power tools, ones without negative side effects or addictive properties.

The major power tool we'll be sharing with you in this section is the power of creative visualization. Throughout the book, you'll find visualization exercises that have been channeled and created to help you move through the various stages of the process of healing yourself of your addiction and creating new life patterns as you move into the future. There are many other power tools to work with, color, sound, and new technological devices like biofeedback machines designed to alter brain waves and body sensations in ways that are at times similar to chemically induced states, but with no dangerous physical effects. See *Megabrain* by Michael Hutchison, (Ballantine Books, 1987) for information on these kinds of power tools.

An Introduction to Visual Meditations

It's no accident that human beings have invented computers. They are, in physical form, perfect diagrams of the functioning of our nonphysical consciousness. Behavior and habits are imprinted on our consciousness much as memory is fed into computers. Once learned, positive habits like brushing teeth and tying shoes need never be changed. Addictions create their own consciousness-imprints.

An alternate power tool we'll be dealing with in this chapter is visual meditation. In India, in addition to the more familiar sound meditations known as mantras, there are also visual meditations known as yantras. Many of these are familiar to us as mandalas. We'll be giving you a number of visual meditation devices that have been channeled to alter consciousness states by looking at them. In this chapter, we'd like to share with you three visual meditations designed to repattern the mind in relation to addictive habits in general.   To use these diagrams, we encourage you to copy them over yourself. They'll have more power if you're looking at an image done in your own hand.

In each chapter on specific addictions, you'll find diagrams designed to clear out and reverse the actual electrical patterns of behavior that flow through and govern addiction to that particular substance. By cleansing and erasing these brain patterns, we are able to release the energy formerly channeled into addiction and use it for more positive purposes. These visual exercises are part of a larger program, including the other exercises in this book, your health care system, and your self-help group.

However, in a sense, these visual meditations are the rock-bottom electrical changes, the rewiring you need. Focus on the diagram for your particular addiction or addictions and follow the directions given. For those who are more oriented toward movement than sight, it may help to trace the pattern in the air, to dance them, or to draw large copies of them over and over again. If you're more oriented toward sound, perhaps you can devise sounds to accompany the movements of your eyes or body, or perhaps you'll find music that seems to go along with them.

Visual Meditations to Change the Pattern of Addictiveness

If you find yourself dependent upon or addicted to a substance, you might want to copy over the following diagram yourself, making it as large or as small as you want. A copy might go on your refrigerator or on your coffee mug, your bar, stash box, or you might want to slip a copy under the cellophane of your cigarette pack, in your wallet or check book.

The function of this first diagram is to help you reprogram your brain so you have more control over your addictive behavior, so your need to be addictive begins to change and diminish. Since it often happens that someone exchanges one addiction for another, this device is another tool to help you step out of addictiveness altogether.

As you look at this diagram, be aware of the triangle moving into the circle, but try to keep your eyes and attention focused on the dot below, in the center of the middle line. The triangle represents the new energy and new living patterns you're inviting into your life. The circle it passes through represents the fullness of your life as you have known it and as it is now. The dot in the center line below the circle is the focal point of this meditation. The three lines represent three deep levels of the subconscious self, and the dot is the seed of transformation emerging into

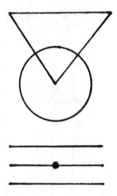

Visual Meditation Device Number 1

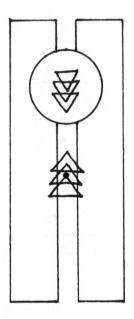

Visual Meditation Device Number 2

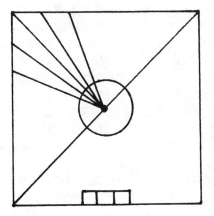

Visual Meditation Device Number 3

consciousness. It represents your capacity to focus and direct your energy, your thoughts, and your will, into recreating the way you live in the world. Think of this diagram as a kind of tai chi for the eyes. Remember that your eyes are dual extensions of your brain, and what you do with them, the things that you see, affect what goes on inside your skull.

The second visual meditation device has another purpose. All addictive substances have negative effects on the physical and energy bodies. As scientists learn more about the brain, they are finding that it is possible to stimulate the brain to release healing substances such as hormones and endorphins. Mystics, yogis, and shamans have known for thousands of years that the mind and the body are not separate. This device is designed to stimulate the brain to speed up and sustain the healing processes of the body. The upper circle is your brain, and the two parallel lines below it are the central energy column of your body. The rectangular lines that connect them remind the eye that what connects inner and outer is the same.

The triple triangles above indicate healing energy, healing substances in the body and in the energy bodies. The triple triangles pointing upward are the outflowing of those energies through the body. They are placed in the area of the chest where the thymus gland is located, which has a major role in the immune system. It's also the location of the newly awakening thymus chakra, called by some the upper heart, high heart, or secret heart. In this diagram you'll be stimulating the brain-thymus connection in yourself and also helping this new chakra to awaken. Its energy is about healing and compassion and planetary peace.

Sit quietly and stare at this diagram. Feel that it's a mirror of yourself. Feel in your brain a movement of healing energy and then feel in your body, at the thymus region, the same movement happening. Focus on the dot in the diagram, and feel in your chest a golden glowing at the equivalent point inside. Sit with this diagram for two or three minutes several times a day. Try to memorize it and how it feels so that you can tune into it without having to look at it, whenever you feel tired, down, in need of a boost of healing energy.

A Visual Meditation for Releasing
Self-Judgment And Moving into the Future

So much guilt, sorrow, anger, resentment and blame get attached to addictions. It's often hard to accept these feelings in ourselves, and it's often hard to learn from them and release them. Addiction can be like a funhouse mirror, distorting everything until we don't know what's real and what's not real. Even after giving up an addictive substance, it can be hard to think of oneself as a regular person, as okay, as anything but a drunk or a drug addict. It's hard to build a sense of self-worth and self-esteem after having been addicted to anything. Sometimes it feels as if you're wearing a sign for everyone to see that says ADDICT. And even if people don't notice it right away, one may wait for them to discover it, or even push them into seeing it in a negative way. It's hard to get to the place where we are coming from our hearts and souls, not just from what we used to drink, smoke, ingest, or inject.

The following diagram, visual meditation device number three was channeled for the purpose of being a stimulus and support for healing and, in the process, for releasing self-judgment and condemnation. Many of you are expecting other people, especially non-addicts, to be almost a different species, ready at every moment to judge and condemn. This device is designed to encourage emotional and spiritual healing. Above all, it's designed to open a doorway in the present to a new way of living, feeling, and moving in the world.   This new approach comes from the joy of being alive, and it invites that feeling in the world to come to us.

You can look at this diagram as often as you like. Draw it and put it anywhere. Your front door or dashboard are good places for it. While the other diagrams are best worked with as black lines on white paper, we encourage you to color in this diagram in any way you like. You might want to make several photocopies and color them differently as you progress. The boxes on the bottom of the diagram are all the things that you have suffered, done, and learned from that can be left behind. The circle and the dot at the center are you, your life, your heart. The lines radiating into and out from the center are all the wonderful, powerful, and healing aspects of life that you can begin to attract to your life, manifest, and share with others. You're already beginning to attract such things, or you wouldn't have this book in your hands, but the diagram will help you speed it up.

Exercises to Heal the Vision of Your Life Task

Earlier we spoke of the problem that arises when a life task or vision is too overwhelming. The teaching exercises which follow are designed to help you become aware of your visions again and start seeing how many possible visions there are. *All* the exercises in this book are designed to help you learn to tap the capacity for vision and use it to heal yourself. Now, you may say that you don't *See* anything, so how can it work? Simply put your imagination to work and don't worry about the results. You don't need to know how to do these exercises any more than you need to know how to digest your food. Something in your brain tells your body how to digest the food. And something in your brain knows how to heal you, if you just tell it you want to do the exercise.

Please note that doing the exercises while you're stoned, drunk, or on a sugar binge would diminish their results and blur the clarity of the vision you're seeking. If you're still actively involved in an addiction, do the exercises when you're as clear as possible, say first thing in the morning. Not only will the exercise work better, but you may also be pleasantly surprised to find the temptation diminished. However, do them any way you can, rather than add them to the endless list of things addicts promise themselves they'll do when they stop.

EXERCISE: For People Who Don't Think They Can Do Visualizations.

1. Sit comfortably in a quiet place. Close your eyes.

2. Become aware of your breathing. Feel your abdomen gently moving in and out for about a minute.

3. Now picture your bedroom in your mind—the furniture, the colors.

4. Now picture the faces of several people you know and care for.

5. Did you "see" your room? Did you "see" the faces? If you didn't get a visual image, at least you knew what they were like. And that's all there is to visualization!

If you find yourself getting stuck as you work through the other exercises, stop, come back and repeat this exercise. Affirm for yourself that you can do visualizations; then go on with the work.

EXERCISE: An Aid to Visualizing

For those who don't feel satisfied with the results of the exercise above, the following exercise will sharpen your visual recall and your experience of visualizations.

1. Sit in front of your television, with the picture turned on but with the sound off.

2. Put your left hand in your lap with the palm up, and press the thumb of your right hand gently into it.

3. Go into a deeper state of consciousness by breathing deeply and slowly, closing your eyes and focusing on the movement of air in and out of the diaphragm.

4. When you feel relaxed, open your eyes and look at the television for a brief moment, and at the same time, press your thumb firmly down into your palm.

5. Now close your eyes. Try to see in detail the exact image you saw on the television screen pressing your thumb into your palm at the same time. Visual memory is stored in the right side of the brain, which also controls the left side of the body. Hence, a strong jab to the left hand linked with a visual impulse which you try to recall a moment later, can serve to stimulate the visual sense.

6. Keep repeating this exercise as often as you need to, until you begin to develop a sense of visual recall. We suggest you use a television so that the image keeps changing, rather than sitting in front of a picture. If you can find a busy street corner or any other place where the image keeps changing, that will work just as well.

7. Whenever you sit down to do a visualization, hold your right thumb lightly on your left palm, stimulating the visualization circuits you've developed through this exercise.

Remember that not everyone is visually oriented and that it's not at all necessary for you to *See* something in order to manifest it, but for some, this increase in visual recall makes the work of this book easier.

EXERCISE: Becoming Aware of Your Vision and Sharing It with the World

Sit quietly and feel your breathing. In the center of your brain, feel a large, golden ball of light, pulsating, warm, and beautiful. Merge your consciousness with that golden sphere. Images, feelings, or ideas may emerge from it, filling you with a sense of purpose. Keep going back into this feeling, and know that it is helping to make your visions conscious in your life again. Soon you will find that this feeling and the sense of purpose which emerges from it are so beautiful you want to share it with everybody. The way to share it is to let it flow out of your body. And the only way to get it out of your body is through a tiny hole in the top of your head. The problem is, how do you do it?

You have options...shrink it down to size, stretch it out, let it drift out like a cloud, melt it and bring it out bit by bit. The tiniest part of the picture contains the whole vision. *Everything Is There* and the capacity to inspire is the same, like a tiny seed that can grow to a whole tree. It is like a hologram, in which any small part can be used to duplicate the whole picture.

EXERCISE: The Wealth of Possible Visions

Sit quietly, feeling your breathing. Become aware of the inside of the body as a dark, open cavern. Around it, there's something very solid that defines its shape, like a mold or plaster cast. The body is full of pure, dark water. At the very bottom, at the tip of the coccyx, which is the floor of the cavern, there is a tiny little spring.

Know that this spring constantly releases a tiny bubble in the darkness—a luminous, golden bubble. It rises up right through the middle of the body and bursts at the top of the head, bursts and falls like shimmering golden stars and disperses in the water. Then another bubble rises up and bursts. Every bubble is different, and each contains a vision (a story, a feeling, a picture, a person). Whether we pay attention to this process or not, these bubbles keep on rising. This is a good exercise to do if you're stuck for inspiration on some work you may be doing, creative or not. It will heal the part of you that looks to a substance for inspiration rather than within.

Addicts lose the memory that the bubbles are always rising—they want to grab a bubble and hold on tight. This exercise puts us back into the ceaseless flow of the bubbles of inspiration. Addicts feel they've only got one bubble. They look at someone who's made it in their field and forget that for each great thing anyone has done, there were many bubbles.

How Thinking Shapes Our Reality
Positive and Negative

This same capacity for vision has other ramifications. We all use our visions to shape our reality—much as the potter uses creative vision to mold clay. It represents a bit of progress today that everyone is familiar with the power of positive thinking. Very few tap into that power—most of us constantly tap into the power of negative thinking—but at least we are beginning to be aware that changing to a positive mental attitude can change our lives in a positive way. Negative attitudes pervade and permeate our world. Just listen to the conversations around you on the bus, on the job, from your neighbors and family—and you see how defeatist the attitudes are. Life is awful; I'll never get ahead; it'll never get better; you cannot beat city hall; do unto others before they do unto you.

Negative thinking affects all of society, but it also affects you personally. For instance, if you go into a job interview convinced you'll make a poor showing and not get hired, your lack of belief in yourself may come across and turn the interviewer off, even when you're qualified. If you have a deep belief that lovers will eventually betray you, your belief may cause you to act suspicious, watchful, and brooding, until finally your lover gets sick of it and says, "I'm tired of your moods. I want out of this relationship," and begins to look for someone else. Then, having had your disbelief in love confirmed, you may go out on a binge.

Negative thoughts repeated through the years become as unconscious a part of ourselves as tying our shoes. Even after an addiction is ended, the negative thoughts can still persist which may have impelled you to the addiction. "I'm just like my father. I'll never do it on my own. I don't deserve to be happy. I might as well go back to drinking, drugging, or overeating." Our addiction to negativity can be even more powerful than our addiction to sugar or tobacco or cocaine.

But it's possible to change the negative patterns through visualizations and affirmations. Use the following exercises to begin the clearing-out process.

EXERCISE: Clearing Out the Negativity

Sit quietly in a bubble. It's murky and grey in there, very depressing to sit in. The greyness is your years of negativity, your years of addiction. You may experience specific images and feelings or just a sense of fog. What is needed is light, so that part of you which knows how to do these things turns it on. A stream of white light begins pouring into the top of the bubble. Little by little, the negativity is dispersed. The grey may not disperse completely the first time you do this. You may need to repeat it again and again, focusing on different issues each time. But eventually, you'll find that you're sitting in a bubble of pure white light, radiantly alive.

If you're more of a sound person than a visual person, you can redesign this exercise and use discordant sounds as the grey fog, sounds you slowly disperse and replace with the music you love. Those who are kinesthetically inclined might work with warmth versus cold or damp air. Whatever works for you and helps you, feel free to use.

EXERCISE: Resisting Negativity From Others

A variation of the exercise above can help when the negativity you need to disperse comes from someone else. This often happens, for example, when you've failed many times in stopping your addiction. Now, when you stop drinking or smoking or when you go on a diet, you're met with spoken and unspoken skepticism from others. One way to combat their negative suggestions is to talk about the positive change you want to make only with people who will be truly supportive, nurturing, and encouraging. That's why a self-help group is an asset in combating all the negativity outside.

In addition, each time the negativity of other people rises up to make you doubt yourself, repeat the following exercise. Go back in the bubble, and become aware of a cloud of greyness that surrounds you on the outside of your bubble. This is the negativity that comes to you from others. It often comes from skeptics or co-addicts who may unconsciously depend on your being addicted to serve their own needs. Feel a great white light surround you and disperse the fog.

Look into the past, too, for ways that other people's negative comments and predictions might still be influencing you, like the way your mom always said you'd never amount to anything. Use this technique on all such potent material from the past. Work with specific individuals, if you need to, each time you do it.

If you're the loved one of an addict and reading this material out of concern for them, you can use this set of exercises to counteract your own negative thoughts about their getting well again. Your negative thoughts can affect them psychically, so it's important for you to change your consciousness about their capacity to stop. Visualize them free of the addiction, happy and healthy, and they will receive this positive thought.

EXERCISE: Building Positive New Thoughts

Naturally, as you work with the two previous exercises, you'll be building positive new thoughts to counteract specific old thought patterns. It's tiring, however, to struggle *Only* with the negative. It's nice sometimes to just start fresh. Put yourself in a bubble and fill it with pink light this time. Select an affirmation of some wonderful new pattern you'd like to promote. "I am lovable, loving, and loved," is a good one for the pink. Or, "I release all obstacles from the past that prevent me from manifesting my life visions."

As another exercise, fill your bubble, your body, and your brain up with this bright glowing pink. It's so full that it overflows and wisps of it start coming out of your heart with each repetition of the affirmation—puffs of pink clouds. The puffs collect and form a dazzling, glowing pink cloud, like the most beautiful sunset cloud display you ever saw. You accept the pink cloud as the affirmation of this beautiful new form you are manifesting in your life, beginning right now.

Using Your Capacity for Vision to Heal Your Addiction

This whole book is about the special ability people who become addicts have to perceive the realms beyond the material. Whether you see these things, hear these things, feel these things, or simply *Know* these things, you're a person with a special gift of vision and a special gift for shaping that vision into form.

The exercises already given and the many further exercises will teach you to use vision to heal yourself and possibly to help other addicted people. You can use them also to unleash your capacity for vision to work creatively or in other ways to make your life fuller and better, without the need to rely on the addictive substance. The following sections will give you more information about planes and realms you've already glimpsed, however dimly. They will also teach you what effects addictions have on other planes and on your bodies which are not tangible, such as the energy body or aura.

Stopping the addiction may not be instantaneous, although for some who've reached their absolute bottom, it may be. Using these exercises does not mean you don't need health care, therapy, or support groups. However, the exercises will help both the abrupt stopper and the tapering-off stopper. Both will doubtlessly struggle with temptation, and each exercise will help with that. Know that temptation can come up at any point in the process, even long after you've actually stopped the addiction. It can be triggered by any stress, and life is full of stresses.

Drink signals, drug signals, or food signals are no more than that. They can be obsessions without being compulsions—you need not act on that old, familiar command. If at any point in the process these signals arise, repeat the exercises in this section. Go back to square one and get a solid foundation beneath you once more before you resume the work of recovery. Use the light tools already given to you as a substitute for your addiction.

Most important of all, do not think that simply because you've stopped, you're now well. You need to work through the entire section and complete all the healing and cleansing exercises—physical, emotional, and spiritual. Otherwise, there is always the danger of slipping back. If you haven't repaired the damage the addiction has done, you cannot come back to health. Health and happiness are our goals here, not a dry or thin or drugfree but miserable human being.

Please note that if you have a serious chemical addiction—many pills or a large quantity of alcohol daily or a dual addiction—you may go through physical withdrawal as you stop, and thus you'll need medical supervision. Withdrawal from a heavy drug or alcohol habit can be a serious matter—convulsions and other complications can result if you try to do it alone. Do not use fear of withdrawal as a reason to keep on—longer addiction can only make it worse—but do get help in going through it.

In all cases, get a checkup. For milder withdrawal, however, avoid tranquilizing medications if at all possible, since they also damage the physical and energy bodies. Whether the withdrawal is mild or severe, it would be helpful to use the bubble of white light, massage, plenty of rest, and herbal teas like fenugreek, parsley, chapparal, and echinacea. (Consult a book on herbology before selecting an herb tea or, best of all, go to an herbologist for invaluable help in this period of recuperation.)

You may ask, what if I've stopped using my major substance—alcohol, drugs, sugar, for example—but I'm still using caffeine, sugar, or cigarettes? I'm not ready to give them up. Can I still use these exercises and be healed? Yes, it's important to begin healing the damage. Strangely enough, as you do these exercises for your main addiction, you may find that, in time, the cleansing and healing allows your lesser addictions to drop away as well.

Ritual—A Helpful Substitute

For our ancestors, life was highly ritualized. The week, the year, the course of a life, were all arranged according to very specific patterns. Daily life was ritualized. Vocations, tools, and household items were passed down from generation to generation. That order, though stifling at times was safer and more comforting than contemporary life with its scarcity of rules to live by. The ritualized aspects of religion are also disappearing.

Many people still desire ritual in their lives, and there's an aspect of addiction that provides it—the habit. Even when the addictive substance is relinquished, the cookie jar is given away, the stash box has paper clips in it, and the mugs are used for sprouting plant cuttings, the need for quiet ritual remains. What follows are several exercises designed to help you create new sets of safe habits that satisfy the ancient need for simple, humble repetitious order in our lives. Try one or all of them, or create one of your own. Use them to help you connect to the world of things and beauty again in a healthy way.

RITUAL ONE:

1. Find an object that connects you to your sense of power. It should be beautiful and healing and should remind you of some part of yourself that is special and that you cherish. It might be a crystal, shell, feather, ring, bracelet, or a carving. If it's small, find or make a pouch for it. If it's larger, find a basket, a box, or a beautiful piece of cloth that you can keep it in. Keep it in a special place.

2. Find a quiet time when you can sit with your special object. You might want to light candles, burn incense, and play some special music. Become aware of your breathing as you build the bubble around yourself.

3. Take your object out of its pouch, box, or wrappings. Feel that you're some kind of priest or priestess handling a sacred object. Hold it, feel it, and caress it with your eyes. Pass it around your body in your bubble. Hold it in front of your heart for a while, and absorb its specialness and sacredness into your heart.

4. Let your special object recharge you and remind you of all the wise, strong, beautiful, and good things that you are.

5. When you feel changed by your time with this object, slowly cover it up again, dissolve your bubble, and put the object away.

6. Whenever you're feeling tired, scared, alone, or disconnected from yourself, take out your object, create your sphere of light, and commune with it again.

RITUAL TWO:

In the Far East, the ceremony of tea is both an art form and a meditation. Think about creating a ceremony for yourself. It will require you to find several beautiful objects—a cup or mug, a vase perhaps, and a teapot. However you structure your ceremony, each object ought to be something that gives you pleasure to see and touch. Instead of your favorite caffeinated brew, substitute something simple and herbal, like peppermint or chamomile.

1. Again, you might want to light a candle, burn incense, and play some special music. Put on a pot of water to boil, as you cut a single flower and put it in your vase.

2. Create your bubble of light around you. Sit quietly and get centered.

3. As you pour the water, be aware of the pot, the steam, the smells, colors and textures. Take pleasure in all of

them. Be as present as you can be when you do this. Feel the heat in the teapot, really notice the pattern on the mug, fully taste the tea.

4. When you've finished as much of the tea as you want, dissolve the bubble.

Do this whenever you need to feel empowered by yourself and your body again, for all ritual connects the mind and body in simple ways. You can do this ritual every morning or every night. Use the energy of your bubble to embrace you and protect you. Use the objects to connect you to the world. Think about all the other people—potters, farmers, shippers, store clerks—who were involved in getting these things to you. Let this ritual weave you into the world and remind you of how you're not alone and isolated, even if you sit on the floor in a corner by yourself. You can do this with spring water or fruit juice or with a loaf of bread or a plate of noodles. Use the same riveted attention you gave to your addiction to focus in on whatever ritual you create.

RITUAL THREE:

In many cultures, a person was encouraged to create a song or dance or painting that celebrated some aspect of his or her life. A hunter returning from a successful hunt might spontaneously create a dance to celebrate. A young woman or man returning from a vision quest might burst into a power song that was theirs alone, that contained the seed and story of their vision, so that whenever they sang it they were empowerd again by the energy of the original experience.

So many of us are disconnected from our own creativity. We turn on the stereo to hear music, but we don't know how to listen to it. We watch a dance concert but never move from our seats to dance ourselves. We stop drawing when we finish elementary school and never draw again, except for the occasional doodle we make while talking on the telephone.

In this exercise we invite you and encourage you to create something that celebrates you, rejoices in you, and connects you back to yourself. It doesn't have to be beautiful or valuable, because the beauty and value aren't in it, but in you and in what it reminds you of. It can be a silly little song you make up in the shower about how good you feel each time you look in the mirror and smile because you're still alive against all odds. It can be a bunch of stick figures drawn with one of your kids' crayons on construction paper that tells the story of something you feel proud of, the day you ran three miles, the night you finished your first project in night school. It can be a dance you choreographed for yourself in the middle of the living room to celebrate the first anniversary of your sobriety. Whatever it is, it's by you and about you and for you.

When is the last time you did something like that—in kindergarten—in a bar one night—or, never? Well now it's time to do it, to create something of power for yourself that comes out of your life and your experiences. Create something you can do when you feel down and out and in need of self-encouragement, and something to do when the spiritual warrior in you needs to celebrate itself. Then, take out your picture or your carving, sing your song, do your dance. Create your bubble around yourself and be light-filled. Do it for yourself and for anyone you want to share it with. Make this your own special piece of magic.

Exercises to Help You Stop Your Addiction

The exercises above were meant to help you find things to replace your habit and the rituals connected with it. The exercises which follow will further help you in the process of stopping.

EXERCISE: Creating the Lock of Intention

If you believe you're going to change, yet find yourself slipping back to old habits, stopping, starting, stopping, starting, taking another cigarette, then you might benefit from this exercise.

Making a cerebral decision isn't enough. The decision has to be made on all levels. Those with energy body damage will have trouble with this decision, hence this exercise. It's designed to help you use your spiritual support system, the one developed in the preparatory section, and to put a lock on your intention at all levels.

1. Begin the exercise by creating your bubble of light and making the contact with your spiritual friends, as you did in Chapter One. Thus your heart center is being nourished by this exercise and you're also beginning to create the lock of intention.

2. When you're able to feel the two-way flow of energy between your heart center and that of your spiritual friends, then put your intention into words. Say something like, "I want to change and I am ready to change." You can make it as short or long as you like. You can include very specific information about what you want to change, or you can just express the desire for change. The important thing is to be clear about your intent and to address your words to the presence of your spiritual friends.

3. Constructing The Energy Lock. Contract the sphincter muscles of your anus. Feel as you do that a flow of energy rises up your spine to your heart center. When it reaches your heart, feel it merge with the energy that travels down to your heart. Feel this union of energies flow outward from you.

4. The friends will support you in this exercise. Their breathing will move with yours. When you do the body lock, they will do it also, stepping up their own energy current. This current will leave their bubble and enter your heart as yours enters theirs. Feel it.

5. Inhale as deeply as possible, and feel that each time you do you draw their energy deeper and deeper into your heart.

6. At the moment you've inhaled so deeply that you feel about to burst, draw into your heart all the energy you can hold. In the moment just before you exhale, bring the curled fingertips of both hands together and tap your chest twice very firmly right over your heart. Then relax your muscles. The tap brings into your physical body the awareness that happened on the spiritual plane. It's the tapping that makes the lock. It's the tapping that locks together your intention and the support of your spiritual companions.

7. In the beginning, you may have to keep repeating the exercise. You may have to do it six to ten times. But at some point, the connection between you and the friends will be so strong that when you need nurturing and when you need the strength to sustain your intention, all you'll have to do is to tap your chest twice over your heart, and the support-energy will flow through.

EXERCISE: Getting the Strength to Remember

Okay, we know what you're asking now—"How do I remember to use the tool? I believe it works, but how do I remember to use it before I eat the chocolate cake or take my partner's cigarette? I always remember the helpful hints later."

In the beginning, you won't consciously remember beforehand, not without willful changes of the energy level. The following exercise is a help for that remembering. Do it in bed, just before falling asleep.

1. Once again, surround yourself with the bubble of light.

2. Mentally create a typical situation in which someone offers you a drink, or cigarette or see yourself taking one.

3. Now, in this imaginary situation, picture yourself about to reach out and take it. Remember that you do not have to take it, and imagine yourself tapping yourself on the chest twice, then saying no. Imagine that in spite of social pressure to take it, you are able to refuse.

4. Feel yourself filling with a good feeling, self-esteem. Feel the whole bubble fill up with good feelings. Smile, inhale, and now tap yourself twice on the chest in actuality.

5. In some way, in words or in feeling, give thanks to your spirit friends for helping you, and then go to sleep.

This visualization is helpful because when you face the situation in real life, it may be difficult to make a clear decision. There is too much talking, pressure, and confusion. The exercise is designed to create an alternate energy current, an alternate energy source of strength to aid us. The more you repeat it before going to sleep, the more the energy will be there for you when you need it. It's carried into the problem situation not by conscious will alone but from deeper, dream-strengthened places as well.

EXERCISE: Healing the Guilt Caused by Slips

Guilt and self-blame are powerful factors in rehooking you on your addiction. We'll deal with toxic guilt over the past, later on. The guilt relevant here is the kind you feel when you once more fall into your addiction. Sometimes, when we take the piece of chocolate cake, drink the glass of wine, or smoke the cigarette, we feel so guilty about having broken our resolution that the only thing that makes us feel better is another piece of chocolate cake, another glass of wine, or whatever the addiction is. Thus a self-perpetuating cycle of guilt and failure can arise, which these exercises are designed to avoid. Guilt is fattening; you can get drunk on guilt.

STAGE ONE: Transmuting the Substance

Love has the power to change or minimize the effects of the addictive substance. Thus, if at this point in time, the temptation is irresistible and you must eat the cake, drink the wine, smoke the cigarette, at least do it with love. Allow yourself to have pleasure in doing it, because pleasure can change it to a lesser poison. Home-made cookies and cakes which are baked with love are less harmful than the machine-made kind, because when we eat them, we also ingest the love the baker brought to the work. Thus, if you're still not at a point where you can resist the cake, wine, or addictive substance, take it in your hands and surround it with a bubble of pink light, sending it love and loving yourself at the same time.

STAGE TWO: Cleansing the Guilt

If you've already taken in the substance you're trying to avoid, this exercise helps in cleansing toxic guilt which might otherwise perpetuate the cycle.

1. Visualize a bubble of white light around yourself, as in other exercises. Energize it, and feel it alive and loving around you.

2. Now let the bubble fill up with the negative feeling you are having about the slip—guilt, remorse, self-blame, or hopelessness. Let it fill the bubble until it's ready to burst.

3. Now imagine that all around the outside of the bubble is falling a soft, golden, healing rain. Hear it pitter-patter softly on the outside of the bubble that surrounds you.

4. Now see it begin to enter the top of the bubble. It drips and falls, draining out the bottom, carrying the dust and litter of your negative feelings away. Just feel the guilt drain away, until all that is left is the golden rain that washes, cleanses, and heals you.

5. Stop the rain and dissolve the bubble.

EXERCISE: Unraveling the Addictive Thread

Sometimes you can have trouble stopping because there is one burning issue in your life, something so close to the surface, so near at hand that every time you take a step, you trip over it. For example, you may be eating, drinking, or drugging to keep your anger down. Or, you may be doing it to drown your sorrow over a love who left you, someone who died, or some major disappointment. Whatever that burning issue is, you'll have work to do to alleviate it through whatever therapeutic or healing modalities you may be using, but first it has to be identified. Sometimes it's quite clear to you—you may know it's because of rage, for example.

Very often, however, the drug is so successful at blunting the feeling that it creates amnesia, and you simply don't know what the feeling is. This exercise is designed to unravel the thread for you. Even if you've stopped, this exercise is valuable for establishing priorities in the healing process. By tackling that issue in conjunction with the cleansing exercises, you'll get relief from it, so there will be less chance of falling back.

The exercise can also be useful to people who have already stopped their addiction but want to get to its roots. It's also good to repeat the exercise at various times in the healing process to get new direction. Priorities will shift from time to time, and there may be periods of confusion where clarity about the process is needed. It will help you decide what to tackle next.

1. Get in your bubble, contact your Core Self, and spend time going into a deeper level of consciousness, letting your breath take you there.

2. Envision an enormous ball of bright blue yarn, which you hold in both hands. Notice that you're at the entrance of a giant maze which represents your addiction.

3. Toss the ball of yarn in front of you, saying "Lead me to the center of my problem." The ball begins to unravel, and you follow it into the maze.

4. The ball unwinds through the many twists and turns of the maze, and you follow it. Now and then the ball will stop in front of a huge blank viewing screen.

5. As you approach the screen, connect with your Core Self and say, "Please reveal to me one small part of the problem." You may see something happen on the screen or you may simply know without seeing. It could be an episode in your life or a typical situation in which the addictive need arises. Thank your Core Self for the information.

6. The ball starts up again and you follow it down the twisting corridors. The ball rolls into another room and stops before another viewing screen. You again ask for a piece of information and you again thank your Core Self for the answer.

7. This happens several times more, the ball of yarn getting smaller, and each screen revealing another small part of the problem or another typical episode.

8. The ball of yarn is nearly gone, when you finally come to the center of the maze and another viewing screen.

9. Sit silently for a moment, reviewing the episodes. Connect to your Core Self with all your heart, and ask to see the cause of your addiction very clearly.

10. An image begins to form and you realize that what you see before you is a mirror. Study yourself in the mirror for a minute, an say, "I see now what needs to be changed. Reveal to me how to change. Give me the strength to change." Send love and compassion to the self reflected in the mirror. Know that the causes are not external but within you, and have to do with the ways to deal with these situations.

11. As you emerge from the maze, thank your Core Self for the information and ask for help and strength in making changes.

Using Affirmations to Repattern Your Thoughts

One of the best tools for changing your thought patterns to reopen to your sense of vision is to work with affirmations. We are so accustomed to thinking negative thoughts, both consciously and unconsciously, that we act out of them without realizing it. We shape our experience of the world by our thoughts, and using affirmations is a powerful way of transmuting our thoughts from destructive ones to life embracing ones. What follows is a list of possible affirmations to work with. Some people find it easier to write them down and others find it easier to say them, either silently or out loud. One powerful method is to repeat your affirmation seventy times a day for seven days. The repetition is part of the mental reprogramming. Keep repeating them during the day and especially as you're drifting into sleep, so they can drift into your unconscious mind also. They may not generate changes overnight, but remember that your negative programming was probably going on for years and years.

1. I release the need for alcohol, drugs, coffee, cigarettes, and other addictive substances.

2. I invite healing into every aspect of my life.

3. I am changing and growing every day.

4. I connect to a Higher Source of love and light.

5. I live in the present and renew myself at each moment.

6. My body is cleansed of all toxins.

7. I release all toxic emotions accumulated throughout my life and learn healthy ways of dealing with emotions in the now.

8. I release all toxic relationships, past and present.

9. I move through the world in new ways, attracting new friends and new experiences into my life.

10. I experience the world as a safe place.

11. I am participating in changing the world.

12. No experience is ever wasted. I learn from everything I think and feel and say and do.

13. I now release the past and move into the future feeling strong, cleansed, and renewed.

14. I forgive myself and others.

15. I love myself and others.

This list is only a small sample of the possible affirmations you can create for yourself. Each one you create can be tailor-made to satisfy a particular day or need. Be inventive in the affirmations you create for yourself. Sit in your bubble, fill your brain with golden light, and feel it pour down from your brain to your throat. As it reaches your throat let it turn into the words that you have chosen to work with, and let the words emerge in sound or through your hand from the luminous depths of your beingness.

CHAPTER THREE

FLOWER POWER REVISITED—FLOWER ESSENCES AS A HEALING TOOL

This is the second of a series of three chapters to introduce you to power tools to replace your substances. You have already begun to work with light. Here we'll introduce you to flower essences, and then they'll be referred to throughout the book. The use of stones will be taught in the chapter which follows. The bibliography in the Appendix lists books for those who wish to learn more about these subjects, since we cannot hope to deal with them in depth here without cutting material related directly to your addiction. Andrew and Donna use different methods in their work, and since Donna uses the essences, she is writing this chapter in the first person.

An Introduction to the Essences

An important element was added to my healing work in 1981, when I was introduced to flower essences, which are also known as flower remedies. These liquid formulas are designed to combat specific emotional and spiritual conditions, such as fear, guilt, resentment, or a sense of inadequacy. They are derived from flowers, trees, and other plants, distilled past the level of chemical potency. There are remedies based on plants and also on gemstones for many fixed emotional patterns which are difficult to eradicate by talk therapy alone, including drug, drinking, or eating disorders. A list of remedies will be given later which are especially useful for addicts, co-dependents, and children of addicts.

Since the first set of 38 remedies was developed by Dr. Edward Bach in the 1930s, they've been clinically tested by the case method, with carefully recorded results. There's also one significant research study, which we'll learn about presently. During the 1970s and 1980s, a number of companies developed and tested additional remedies, so that there are now several hundred flower and gem remedies available.

It's important to understand that flower essences and gem remedies do not purport to cure addictions, for addiction is a complex problem requiring many kinds of healings on many different levels. What the remedies are especially good for are repairing damage done to the subtle bodies by addiction, since they work most strongly on the subtle body level. They work particularly on the emotional body, helping the recovering addict who has used substances as tools for coping with or repressing strong feelings. As the substance ceases to work, or as the addict puts it aside, many suppressed feelings will come to the surface. The remedies are tools for cleansing accumulations of emotions, healing the patterns of reaction which accompany them, and increasing conscious awareness both of these feelings and of new ways to cope with them.

Research Demonstrating Their Effectiveness

An extremely well-designed study to test the effectiveness of Dr. Bach's remedies was done by Dr. Michael Weisglas for his doctoral dissertation. He wished to find out whether the remedies were working only through the strength of belief, in a placebo effect. He first gave a series of psychological tests to three groups of people. One group was given an amber dropper bottle with nothing more than spring water and brandy—the placebo. The second group was given an identical bottle with spring water, brandy and four of the remedies. The third group was given the same setup with seven of the remedies. Since the remedies themselves are preserved in brandy, they all tasted and looked exactly alike. It was a double-blind study, meaning that the people who distributed the bottles did not know if they contained the placebo or the real thing.[1]

The three groups were retested with the same psychological examinations after they had taken the remedies for three weeks, and again after six weeks. The tests showed that the group which had the placebo made no significant improvement, while the other two groups showed significant increases in self-awareness, self-confidence, well-being, vitality, and creativity. The group with seven remedies in the bottle, however, experienced more stress and had more of a tendency to drop out of the study. This finding suggested that no more than three or four remedies can comfortably be given without cross-interference.

How to Use Flower Essences

The remedies come in small stock bottles of concentrate, of which three drops are added to a one-ounce amber dropper bottle filled with spring water. A teaspoon of brandy or apple cider vinegar can be added to the diluted mixture as a preservative. Generally, the person takes four drops of the mixture four times a day, with rising and bedtime being especially helpful. By taking them before sleep, the dream life is mobilized for problem solving. Several bottles of diluted mixture might be needed to change a long-ingrained habit, but the day comes when you realize you're different.

In order to find out which remedies are good for you or the addicted person at this stage of recovery, read the descriptions given here and in the books listed in the bibliography. Choose a number which appear to be appropriate. Contact the Core Self of the person and ask, "Is this remedy helpful for _____ at this particular time?" You may get the answer intuitively, yet it's better to check in another way. Some healers use muscle reflex testing, asking the person to hold the bottle of concentrate and raise one arm, keeping it as firmly in place as possible. Attempt to push the arm down, and if the remedy is not the right one, the arm will collapse. Others use a pendulum to test for the remedy, first determining how the pendulum swings for YES and how it swings for NO, and then asking if the remedy is helpful for the person at this time.

After you have made your selection, be sure to test the total combination, as well as the individual remedies, to see if the remedies combine in a way that is helpful at the present time. Certain remedies, such as BLEEDING HEART, evoke such a strong catharsis that they're better taken alone. In addition, the healing process evoked by a particular remedy may work at cross purposes with the process evoked by another; each of them may be good for the person, but they may not be good in combination.

In preparing diluted bottles of remedies for recovering alcoholics, use apple cider vinegar rather than brandy as a preservative, because the taste of the brandy could be difficult to deal with. The remedies themselves are preserved in brandy, so for alcoholics, test to see how many drops of each concentrate to put in the bottle. When done this way, it does not generally bring up drink signals. The amount of brandy is quite tiny—three or four drops to several hundred drops of water.

There are those, however, who are reluctant to take alcohol into their system in even this miniscule amount. For those people, it's just as helpful to put the essences into the bathwater, about seven drops to a tubful of water. In fact, for all who use the essences, this is a most pleasurable and powerful way of absorbing them. A long hot bath with essences, a candle burning, and meditation cleans the aura and gives you a wonderful and refreshing new lease on life.

The Healing Crisis as Related to Essences

We have spoken in a number of places about the various kinds of healing crises connected with addiction and with the efforts you may make to heal yourself. In a later chapter, we'll discuss the specific healings that often accompany the path of recovery from addictions, as emotions which have been long suppressed come to the surface. As we'll see, there are remedies to help cleanse each of these emotions and to change the patterns of thought and behavior which evoke them.

First, however, it would be wise to mention that, like all forms of healing you may undertake, the essences themselves can precipitate their own form of healing crisis. When you take a remedy, let's say for anger, you may actually go through a few days to a week where the anger appears to be worse than ever.   This, however, is in the nature of a catharsis, after which there is relief. It's almost like the spiking of a fever, which is in itself a sign the body is fighting off disease. Likewise, when you take a remedy, your subtle bodies are fighting off and releasing the diseased attitudes and emotions they took on in the course of the addiction. When essences for a particular issue are combined with the exercises for that same issue, the healing is stronger and more complete.   But the catharsis may also be stronger.

Another reason the problem can appear to be worse when you first start a remedy is that these essences work by bringing to the surface patterns of thought and feeling that were previously hidden from your awareness. For instance, your dreams may become quite intense and directly related to the issue at hand. This upsurge of feelings is true for all of us, and yet many who were addicted have used the substance to hide from feelings and conflicts. Those who grew up with addicted parents were especially programmed from the earliest years not to feel. Thus, when feelings start coming to the surface, signals to drug, drink, or overeat may temporarily increase, and you'll doubtlessly need other supports to resist them.

Remember that you don't have to go through this alone. Sharing these feelings with others, such as your self-help group, therapist, sponsor, family, or friends is very important, both for the relief of being heard and for feedback on these old patterns.   (This advice is valid, naturally, for many forms of healing.)

When you've truly hit bottom, your original drug of choice is no longer an option.   But the addictive personality is adept at switching addictions to cover feelings. Thus, your liver may no longer tolerate alcohol, but you may find yourself going on sugar binges, suddenly smoking an extra pack a day, or using your credit cards compulsively. To maximize the healing from the remedies, allow yourself to feel these feelings, rather than run to a new addiction.

Luckily, these upsurges are not long-lasting, so ride them out. Cry or rant and rave if you need to, to get it out of your system. Be gentle with yourself. As you continue to take the remedies, you'll notice a change. You start to become hyperaware of thoughts and patterns of behavior in that area of life, and you grow in your capacity to stand back and observe yourself. As the weeks go on, you'll get sick and tired of some of your old ways of reacting. They'll seem immature or even slightly embarrassing, and before you know it, you've changed. After a while, you may not even remember that you used to react that way, until something comes up that used to be a trigger for an upset, and you're surprised to find it didn't bother you at all.

In general, the addictive person believes that if one is good, seven must be better. There's a temptation to cram as many remedies as possible into the bottle or to take remedies every waking hour. This can stem from a zeal to get better in a hurry—wanting to do it all at once and winding up overwhelming yourself. Recall that Dr. Weisglas' study showed that the group getting seven of the remedies did not do as well as the group receiving only four. The addictive personality has trouble with moderation; you can have too much of a good thing. You also need to take breaks from time to time and use no remedies at all for six weeks or longer. Similarly, you may need vacations from all healing efforts to give your body, mind, and spirit time to assimilate what you've learned.

Remedies to Help the Addict and Co-Dependent

Hundreds of remedies are available, but the ones listed in this chapter are those which would be especially helpful to addicts and those who love or work with them. The descriptions shouldn't be considered the full range of potential uses of a given remedy, only the specific way it would be useful to people with these problems. Many of the issues we've already covered, such as the vision, are addressed, as well as patterns common to recovery and to the addictive personality. In other chapters, remedies specific to the issues or substances at hand will be given, but the ones here are more related to general issues of addictions.

A few remedies will be mentioned which are made from gems, using a similar process to those made from flowers and other plants. There are entire kits of such essences and there are two books by Gurudas, *Gem Elixers and Vibrational Healing, Vol. I and II* which detail their use. I worked with gem elixers early on, but now only use RUBY, TURQUOISE, ROSE QUARTZ, and OPAL. The reason is that the healing crisis evoked by gem elixers seems much stronger and more cathartic than those evoked by flower remedies. Especially in combination with the exercises, the crisis seemed too painful and difficult for the recovering addict. Gentleness is indicated in recovery, even for those inclined to tough it out. Harder is not necessarily better. For others not so damaged by addictions, the gem elixers may be useful, but I do not recommend them for most recovering addicts.

Categories of Essences

Listed below are a number of remedies helpful with the dimensions of addiction we've already discussed, such as the vision of the life task. There are a variety of remedies under each category, for example for grounding. Each is distinctly different, yet for me to describe them in detail would take too long and detract from our primary purpose. If you're not certain which of several remedies listed applies to you at this time, consult the sources in the bibliography. Also use a pendulum or muscle testing.

Bottoming Out And Discouragement About Stopping

BORAGE eases discouragement at relapse and gives you the courage to keep working on your addiction or on manifesting your vision. CAYENNE helps you let go of deeply ingrained habits like addictions and catalyzes quick change and growth, when you feel stuck in a particular pattern. CHESTNUT BUD lets the addict or co-dependent learn from mistakes, rather than repeating the same unproductive patterns over and over. CRAB APPLE heals the addict's self-loathing and guilt, as well as the feeling of being sick and tired of being sick with the disease. GOLDENROD BUD helps with the sense of being powerless. GORSE is for chronic problems like addiction, relieving the sense of hopelessness from having failed so many times at stopping the addiction.

PENNYROYAL is extremely useful to addicts and those who live or work with them, in that it acts against negative thinking and shields you from negative psychic bombardment. It's a specific against abuse of alcohol and other drugs. SWEET CHESTNUT is for those who are in great anguish and have reached the limit of their endurance, yet who are not suicidal. Those who are bottoming out could use it to move forward into recovery. WILD ROSE remotivates those who have become totally resigned to their addiction and who apathetically accept their enslavement.

Grounding And Clarity

CLEMATIS works to ground the addict in reality, and to overcome the need to live in a dream world and be spaced out all the time. LOTUS is said to be a master healer and general spiritual tonic which helps meditation, mental clarity, and emotional balance. MANZANITA helps you become grounded and at home in the physical body. OPAL is a gem essence which specifically gives clarity to those coming off addictions, relieving fogginess, reestablishing structure, and releasing hopelessness. SQUASH also helps you feel grounded.

Alienation And Isolation

HEATHER relieves the loneliness and self-centeredness that arises when addiction has shrunk your world down to the size of a bottle or pill. MARIPOSA LILY heals the feeling of alienation which accompanies the progression of an addiction. SHOOTING STAR is a tool against the alienation often felt by those whose vision is an unusual one. If you feel that earth is not your home, this may be the remedy for you. WALLFLOWER is good for those who have to drink, drug, or overeat in order to dance, attend social functions, or approach a possible date. It helps restore confidence in your attractiveness. WALNUT is for the hermit or isolated person who stays aloof from people, then abuses substances to cope with the loneliness.

Help With Manifesting The Vision

BLACKBERRY helps people who are overwhelmed by their visions and doubtful of their ability to manifest them. BEECH is for those who are too critical and demanding of themselves and others and also for the perfectionism which is a primary problem with many substance abusers. CALIFORNIA POPPY works on creative blocks and on bringing about spiritual balance. ELM relieves the feeling many capable people have of being inadequate to their tasks and to their visions, a feeling they may abuse substances as power tools to overcome. GENTIAN is good for self-doubt and the negative outlook of people who get discouraged easily and quit.

INDIAN PAINTBRUSH helps the addict develop a greater frustration tolerance. It's also good at revitalizing creative abilities which might have gone dormant in the course of the addiction. IRIS is an incredible remedy for freeing creativity and for relieving frustration about realizing your vision. LARCH helps when you expect to fail at your vision, so you don't even try. It relieves despondency and the inferiority complex. MADIA lets the addict, recovering or otherwise, focus on tasks, attend to detail, and follow through on commitments. The combination of BLACKBERRY, IRIS, and MADIA is an excellent power tool for manifesting your visions and goals, especially in the creative realm.

MULLEIN is for the problem of having a vision which is very unusual or very difficult, for it lets you be true to yourself and fulfill your true potential. OAK is a balm for those who drink, overeat, or abuse pills to compensate for a lifetime of hard struggle. PENSTEMON is one of the stronger remedies against discouragement and self-doubt, effective with those who are overwhelmed by challenges. WILD OAT is related to the vision and to dissatisfaction at not having discovered or pursued it. Often multi-talented, these people have not found their niche in life.

Other Addictive Patterns

AGRIMONY offsets the tendency addicts and their families have to hide their suffering behind a facade and then use the substance to cover the feelings over. IMPATIENS relieves the irritability of the nervous system which arises with substance abuse and is good for impatience. MORNING GLORY helps with general compulsivity and with certain kinds of habits. I haven't found it useful in relieving overeating, but it's worth a try, for it may affect different people in different ways. ST. JOHN'S WORT opens you up to a loving, trusting connection with a Higher Power, when the addiction has made you loose faith. It also relieves troubled dream states and releases fears. SWEET PEA is for the defiant, antisocial, acting-out type of addict, especially the teenager or young adult. WHITE CHESTNUT relieves mental obsessions, worries, and the racing of the mind that many people use substances to shut down.

Co-dependency And Adult Children
Of Alcoholics

CENTAURY may be useful for the co-dependent in overcoming the pattern of being exploited or victimized. For the addict, it strengthens the will. CHICORY is for the co-dependent who is determined to set the addict right, often becoming a martyr in the process. GOLDEN EARDROPS is excellent for those who grew up in alcoholic or dysfunctional households, for it helps you gain perspective on these unhappy memories and release repressed sorrow. MARIGOLD is very effective with those from such backgrounds in healing early emotional traumas.

POMEGRANATE heals emotional extremes due to lack of childhood nurturing. RED CHESTNUT is invaluable for the co-dependent who feels the need to rescue people. It relieves the tendency to be excessively anxious and overprotective of others. RED CLOVER is useful for anyone who works or lives with addicts, in that it keeps you centered at the height of the emotional drama around you. SAGEBRUSH would be excellent for adult children of alcoholics and other dysfunctional families in that it helps you cast off parental programming and be true to yourself, finding your own identity. VINE is excellent for co-dependents who've become excessively controlling or dominant as a result of coping with an addict. YARROW builds the psychic shielding needed for protecting those who are around addicts. For addicts, it also protects against the temptations offered by drinking buddies and others who will you into addiction.

Essences Of General Usefulness
Which You May Want To Incorporate

CHAMOMILE is soothing in essence form, even more so than in herb tea. It calms you down and relieves confusion and stress, bringing emotional objectivity. QUARTZ lessens emotional extremes, calms the energy body, and helps with meditation. PEACH should be tested to add to other combinations as it's said to reduce healing time by amplifying other remedies. RESCUE REMEDY should be part of any first aid kit, for all those involved in any physical or emotional crisis. (It's made up of a combination of remedies.) SELF-HEAL activates the innate ability of the mind, body, and spirit to heal itself. STAR OF BETHLEHEM heals shocks and traumas, of which there are many in the lives of addicts and their loved ones. No matter how long ago it happened, the energy body may still be contracted in reaction, so test for this remedy whenever there have been serious traumas in the person's life. ZINNIA is a gift to the child within, releasing laughter and playfulness. When you're working too hard at healing yourself or others, treat yourself to this one.

As you read through this list and lists in other sections, you may very well find that the essences of flowers, trees, and other plants you've always loved—or hated—have a special healing meaning for you. In recovery, you may have developed a fondness for the comfort of chamomile tea, and now you discover that the essence CHAMOMILE has a soothing and calming effect, even stronger than the tea. Perhaps you've always adored willow trees, and you find that WILLOW, the essence, helps heal bitterness. On an intuitive level, many of us have strong reactions to the vibrations of plants, even though we aren't conscious of their purpose. What does it mean, for instance, that we associate holly with Christmas, when the essence HOLLY is used for healing so many difficult problems in human interactions? As one clue to choosing essences that may be especially good for you, look up the meaning of the essences of your favorite flower, jewel, tree, houseplant, and spice.

Examples of How the Remedies Are Used

In my work with recovering addicts and their families, I use a combination of exercises and essences, as the combination is far more effective at cleansing toxic emotions.   In Chapter Six, you'll be given specific exercise and remedy combinations for such major emotional cleansings as guilt, fear, rage, and resentment. We'll also talk about the predictable emotional crises of recovery. Here, however, it would seem meaningful to give some case examples of how the essences are used and of the typical layers that come up one after another. The order of the layers and the intensity with which they emerge vary with the individual. (In these examples, the client's identity is disguised.)

Trudi had a long history of sugar binges and took diet pills to keep her weight down. However, on her 22nd birthday, on the way home from a party given for her, she was raped. From that point on, she needed to drink and take drugs to go out with men or to a party, and the problem with binges intensified. After being in Overeaters Anonymous for a year and then putting the drugs and alcohol down as well, the terror about the rape five years earlier came to the surface very strongly as her birthday approached. She came to me, having heard of some of the "strange" things I was doing with people Trudi knew.

We first tackled the panic attacks with a combination of the exercises to be given in Chapter Six and essences related to fear. STAR OF BETHLEHEM is important in releasing the shock of any major trauma, no matter how long ago. ROCK ROSE is for panic and terror. MIMULUS is for specific fears. After working with the remedies and exercises for fear for a while, a layer of shame and guilt, all too common to the crime victim, emerged. Trudi began to reproach herself, saying she must have caused it somehow. I suggested she talk to the rape counseling center, even though it had happened several years earlier, to get some perspective on the feelings common to victims of rape. I also taught the exercises for guilt and gave Trudi the essences PINE for guilt, CENTAURY for those who have been victims, and CRAB APPLE for self-loathing and the sense of being somehow dirty.

Quite quickly, a layer of rage emerged, which Trudi courageously lived with for several weeks without resorting to her addictions. Exercises for anger and resentment were needed, as well as the essences VERVAIN, for those who are incensed at injustices, WILLOW for resentment, and HOLLY for hatred and the desire for vengence. The final layer which emerged had to do with the damage to her sexuality, so the sexual part of her energy body was cleansed and strengthened by exercises presented in the second book and by such essences as STICKY MONKEYFLOWER, FIG, and HIBISCUS, all related to sexual dysfunction. As time went on, Trudi was able to date again without resorting to alcohol, drugs, or overeating.

Not only does the order of the layers vary for the individual, but the length of time each remedy is needed also varies. For instance, one woman who'd been violent during her drinking and who still punched holes in walls in sobriety was given a single remedy, CHERRY PLUM. By the time the bottle was two-thirds empty, she found she was able to anticipate the rages, go away to cool off, and then return to deal with the situation. The pendulum indicated that she didn't need a second bottle.

By contrast, a young man with a lengthy history of drug and alcohol addiction was tormented, even after several drugfree, sober years through A.A. and therapy, with the compulsion to make lists in his head and go over them all day long. He was given WHITE CHESTNUT, two, three, and four bottles of it with no relief. He was not in treatment with me, so none of the exercises were used. Although I was ready to give up, he persevered and took a fifth bottle, and at that point, the obsession was lifted permanently. It's rare for a symptom to persist for that long. Since I use a variety of methods and also strongly advocate the Twelve Step programs, it's often hard to say which element is producing the result. In these two cases, however, it's clear that the remedy did what therapy and A.A. had not achieved in the relief of these two symptoms.

Sometimes the addiction is not the main complaint, but is only revealed in the process. Wilson, a black man in his late twenties, came to me first through my astrology practice. His complaint was that he seemed to be stuck in his job in an insurance company and he couldn't motivate himself toward his goals or finish the last few credits toward his degree. He loved the meditations and quickly revealed his own buried psychic gifts.

The first step was to strengthen the solar plexus, the seat of self-worth and self-confidence, through the exercises in the next book in this series, and through such essences as SUNFLOWER, for self-worth, LARCH, for those who are afraid to fail so therefore do not even try, and SAGEBRUSH, for releasing his identification with his father's feelings of failure, racial oppression, and of being held back as a black man in a white society. SAGEBRUSH is often essential for the upwardly mobile who are in pain or conflict about leaving their roots behind. After some months of treatment with these and other remedies, Wilson said that, oh, by the way, he had stopped smoking grass. He hadn't mentioned his daily pot habit before, but had stopped as the course of treatment progressed.

The flower remedies can also be very helpful for the co-dependent. Jill was the adult child of an alcoholic father and came to me because she felt she was "having a nervous breakdown" when her lover, Maureen, went back to drinking alcohol after several years of sobriety in A.A. Although RESCUE REMEDY can be useful in any crisis, in this circumstance, I made a concoction I call the RESCUER'S REMEDY. It consists of PINE, for the feeling of somehow being responsible for another's problems, RED CHESTNUT, for being overanxious and overprotective toward others, CENTAURY, for not being taken advantage of, and RED CLOVER for remaining centered when others are in crisis. This first aid helped Jill calm down enough to take stock of the situation. At my urging, she went to Alanon and also continued to take the combination. Very soon, she was feeling peaceful and was dealing differently, not only with Maureen, but with her still actively alcoholic father.

1 Michael Weisglas, "Bach Flower Essence Research: A Scientific Study," The *Flower Essence Journal*, I (1980), 11-14.

CHAPTER FOUR

STONES—A VIABLE ALTERNATIVE TO GETTING STONED

An Introduction to Crystals

Crystals are among the finest of the earth's natural power tools. They are quite capable, with a little attunement to them, of making the same shifts in consciousness that drugs, alcohol, and other ingestible substances do. In fact, one of our clients, Nora, was given an assignment by one of our guides to meditate while holding a stone and explore why the word *Stoned* is used to describe the sensation drugs give you. You might profitably undertake the same assignment yourself. The beauty and power of crystals can be addictive too, but with few dangerous side effects. Some people may become too spacy from prolonged exposure to them, but such spaciness does not compare to cirrhosis or heart and lung ailments.

Crystal, the stone, should be distinguished from the beads or pendants made from sparkling faceted glass, sometimes called lead crystal. The glass is often quite beautiful, but it has no real healing power. Stone crystals are concentrated aspects of Earth-energy, each one vibrating on and resonating with a different frequency. Clear quartz crystals are used in watches, radios, and computers. Their molecular structure carries an electrical charge.

There are many excellent books available on crystals and crystal healing, and several of them are listed in the bibliography in the Appendix. The primary reference work on stones used in preparing this chapter is the excellent *Crystal Enlightment,* by Katrina Raphaell. (Aurora Press, 1985) There are also many knowledgeable crystal healers giving workshops on how to use them. If we had to mention just one or two whose work has been influential, it might be the Native American shaman, Oh Shinnah, or the scientist, Marcel Vogel. You might look on bulletin boards in your local health food store or New Age bookstore for workshops in your area. It is not our intention in this book to duplicate any of that material, but we do want to share with you several crystal uses that have bearing on the healing of addictions. Later, you'll find specific crystal patterns to use in relation to specific substances. In this chapter, we'd like to give several ways to use crystals to work with addictive problems in general.

Crystals as Power Tools

Crystals aren't magic. They won't change you overnight. But they are another tool, a subtle but strong one you can use as you heal yourself of your addiction. A power tool is designed to alter brain waves, to induce in its user altered, expanded states of consciousness. The problem with alcohol and drugs is that they remain in the system, like a carpenter who can never put his saw down. It's hard to wash dishes or make love when you're holding a saw.

Crystals are capable of doing the same work that chemical power tools do, but you can put them down. You have control of them, they don't gain control over you. It takes far more work at developing your sensitivity to feel the effects of a crystal than it does a glass of wine or a joint or a brownie, but that work is ultimately healing and useful. A crystal habit is far better for you than a drug habit, and over time, not nearly as expensive, either in money or other kinds of costs.

In each chapter dealing with a substance addiction in the second book, you will be given an exercise where you hold one kind of stone in your left hand and a different kind in your right. The kinds of stones are different for each addiction. By holding two different crystals in your hands and deepening your awareness into them, letting their energy wash through you and move you, you can create excellent substitutes for addictive substances. The cerebrum of the human brain is composed of two hemispheres. Each has slightly different ways of processing information. The right hemisphere, which controls the left side of the body, is more fluid, spatial, and visually oriented. The left hemisphere, which controls the right side of the body, is more linear, time-oriented, and verbal. By holding a different stone in each hand and working with the pair, you can subtly alter your brain functions and initiate different states of consciousness.

The gems named in this chapter refer to the actual physical stones. This is because we feel that most recovering addicts will work better with the physical stones than with gem elixirs.

How to Choose Stones for Healing Work

Read about crystals if you haven't already. If you haven't worked with them, the best place to begin is to go to a crystal store, a rock and mineral shop, and just let yourself wander around, looking at and holding different stones. Trust the intuitive part of you that will take you to the crystals you need to work with. All AMETHYSTS are not created alike, nor all QUARTZ crystals, or any other stone. Some are flawed, perhaps wounded by the way they were gathered by humans, and some will fit your own personal need better than others. See what changes they bring forth in you, as you hold these stones and let yourself merge with them. Think of them as food for the spirit.

At first it may be difficult to feel the energies of the stones. It takes a certain amount of sensitizing to be able to do that. Let your hands reach out from deep within you. Think of the stones as living, almost like pets. Their vibrations may be very slow, but when you hold them and think of them as living creatures, you may find it easier to feel them, more like holding a kitten or a baby bird. You may want to put your bubble around you as you make your choices. Later, when you get home, sit in your bubble again and feel that when you hold your crystal you can breathe its energy through your hands into your body.

As more and more people become aware of the use of crystals, the price goes up. The stones you choose need not be expensive ones. They can be uncut and unpolished, rather than gemstone quality. In many such stores, you'll find bins, baskets, or drawers of inexpensive stones, perhaps a lump of SMOKY QUARTZ, EMERALD, or AMETHYST for under a dollar. Again, attune yourself to the stone and let the choice come from an intuitive place, rather than necessarily being influenced by looks. One caution is in order, in that if you're not buying from a known and reputable dealer or from one who is aware of the healing uses of stones, you may be fooled by stones which are color enhanced for more brilliance. ROSE QUARTZ, in particular, is subject to this kind of deception. CITRINE and SMOKY QUARTZ are often heated or irradiated AMETHYSTS or CLEAR QUARTZ, so make sure you ask about the stones you buy.

Cleansing Your Crystals

Because of their ability to hold a charge, crystals do take on the energy around them. They are excellent shields against the vibrations of other people, so many people wear them whenever they are in crowded, public places, in emotionally charged atmospheres, or when they do healing work. However, they need to be cleansed regularly of the vibrations they've soaked up, or they lose their effectiveness and clarity. When you become sensitized to them, you'll begin to know when they are tired and in need of cleansing. They also, as self-preserving living beings, will find a way to hide from you or get lost altogether if they're being overused or not cared for properly. (Like other teachers and guides, however, they may also leave, not because you've abused them, but because you've learned all they have to teach you.) If this sounds like anthropomorphization, wait until you get to know them better.

When you first purchase or receive the crystal, it will need a major cleansing for a week or longer to purify it of all influences other than your own. You may do this by burying it in loose earth or sand, placing it in spring water in the sunlight and moonlight, or soaking it in spring water containing sea salt or RESCUE REMEDY or QUARTZ essence. Do not use sea salt for colored crystals, as it leaches the color out over time. Then from time to time, especially in periods of heavy use or intense healing work, cleanse them again by soaking them or burying them overnight or longer.

Since crystal works on intention, you can also cleanse it by holding it in your hand, visualizing it as clear, and then exhaling quickly and strongly, and feeling that the energy of the breath shoots through your body, arm, and hand, into the crystal and through it, cleansing it. Passing it through a flame or through the smoke of incense as you state your intention that it be cleansed also helps.

Programming Your Crystal for Your Own Purposes

The word "crystal" often refers to the six-sided CLEAR QUARTZ crystal. Its size and clarity vary from piece to piece, but in function, it remains the same. CLEAR QUARTZ is the best tool to use in meditation and self-attunement. Old style psychics and mediums made use of a crystal ball for this reason. Some crystal healers work with no other stones. The regularity of its structure helps support us in restructuring our lives. Its clarity and beauty remind us of our potential. Its solidness helps us become more solid in our lives.

By holding your crystal and rubbing it, you spark the electrical charge quartz crystals hold. Crystals can be programmed much the way computers can. This can be very useful for recovering addicts, as the crystal can become both something physical to hold on to to replace your mug, cigarette, roach clip, or other paraphernalia; and it can also support you in your healing process. For example, you could program a piece of CLEAR QUARTZ to support you in doing a particular exercise in this book. (The first ritual in Chapter Two would be a way of doing that.)

There are many ways to program a crystal. First make sure it's thoroughly cleansed of all other vibrations. Then, you may sit and hold it, visualizing the information you want to put in it. Or you may repeat the words of how you want it to help you. For example, you could say over and over again, "This crystal supports me in visualizing the bubble of energy around me." You could do this until it feels charged, maybe as though it were tingling, or you can use your breath again to charge it. Send the energy of a breath through it to lock the thought or words in. Others pass it through a flame, incense, or burning sage while concentrating strongly on the purpose they intend to use the stone for. Some people write what they want the crystal to help them do on a piece of blank paper and wrap it around the stone for a few days until the information is absorbed.

As with cleansing your crystal, any and all of these methods will work, so use the one you're most drawn to or invent one. For example, if you've chosen to program it to support you in constructing your bubble of white light, hold it every time you sit down to visualize, rub it, and soon you'll begin to feel its effect. When you want to change the program in your crystal, clean it out and program it again.

Various Other Healing Stones

In addition to working with CLEAR QUARTZ, there are several other stones you may find useful in your recovery process. Later in this chapter and in the chapters on specific substances in the second book, we'll mention crystal patterns using several different stones. But if we were to create a medicine chest specifically for addicts, it would have CLEAR QUARTZ in it, as well as the following stones:

Dark green TOURMALINE is one of the great cleansers of the crystal realm. It is excellent for grounding and for dealing with practical issues of survival. It can also be used as a kind of energy vacuum cleaner. Much negativity is carried by addicts and directed at them. You can use a chunk of dark green TOURMALINE of any size to help you clean out your energy field. Stand in the middle of a room with the stone in your hand. Imagine the outer edges of your aura, and spin the TOURMALINE all around you from head to toe. Bring it behind your back, around your arms and legs. This stone will clean your energy field and then clear itself out. It will suck up all the negative energy and transmute it into pure energy again.

RHODOCHROSITE is a beautiful reddish or pink stone that has an affinity for addicts and vice versa. A polished piece of it is a nice companion for your pocket. RHODOCHROSITE helps integrate mind, emotions, and body. It helps you connect your spiritual self and your day-to-day life. It's warm in color and warming to the eyes and spirit. All the imbalances of addiction and the recovery process make this an excellent tool to work with.

ROSE QUARTZ is the stone of love. All the problems on this earth may stem from lack of love, inability to express love, and inability to feel it. Certainly trouble with love is a major component of all addictions. Wearing a ROSE QUARTZ pendant or a string of the beads around your neck, hanging over the heart, can help balance out and heal this problem.

Many addicts are either running from their visions or running in search of them. All this running can leave one ungrounded, like a rolling stone, disconnected from life and the world we live on. Iron PYRITE, which glitters and looks like gold, is a wonderful grounding stone to keep with you for those times when you need to have both feet planted firmly on the ground. It's called fool's gold, but there's nothing foolish about it. There's a fool in every addict. But as we know from folk tales, it's always the king's fool at court who speaks the truth no one else knows, in a way that makes everyone laugh. Many addicts fear that "the straight life" will be dull and lifeless. This stone can help you remember to be in your body with a smile.

Ultimately, however, a recovering addict's best friend may be a piece of AMETHYST—in fact, it's legendary as a remedy against alcoholism. The beautiful purple or lavender stone has the capacity to channel in spiritual energy, support the process of transforming old beliefs and thought patterns, balance out your energy, and support you in meditation. You may want to lay it on your third eye when doing certain of the exercises in this book. It's also a wonderful stone to sleep with; hold it in your hand, tape it to a part of your body, or put it under your pillow or under your bed. If you're still addicted to your major substance—or if there's a minor habit you wish to let go of—you might want to put some AMETHYST chips in your bottle of vodka, your coffee cannister, your cigarette pack, your pill bottle, or your sugar bowl to help transmute the energy of the substances you take into your body.

In addition to these stones, there are several others that you may want to put in your medicine chest or traveling doctor's bag, or in a leather pouch around your neck. BLOODSTONE and AVENTURINE are excellent stones to speed up the body's healing process. SODALINE is good to use if you're afraid of the physical damage you might have caused during your addiction. TURQUOISE is a fine tool for helping to stabilize your emotions, and AMBER will help reattune you to the planet's own energy.

A Crystal Pattern to Normalize Your Brain Waves

All of us have a kind of "home base" pattern of brain waves, a middle range, that addictive substances alter. When that happens, we walk around saying things like, "I haven't been myself lately." That feeling occurs whenever we get disconnected from our home consciousness. Because chemical substances remain in the system for a long time, they continue to alter brain waves for a long time. It is hard to have a a clear consciousness base in yourself when you are healing yourself of your addictions. The following crystal pattern is designed to bring that home frequency back into strength and clarity.

For this pattern you'll need three stones: a piece of CLEAR QUARTZ, a piece of SMOKY QUARTZ and a piece of LAPIS LAZULI. These pieces may be rough or tumbled, pointed or not pointed. They don't need to be much larger than an inch long to be effective, but trust yourself to use whatever size stones you are drawn to. Cleanse the stones in whatever way you're used to, or choose one of the methods taught earlier in this chapter.

Lie quietly, burn some incense, do whatever you do to relax now—deep breathing or soaking in a tub. Stretch out in a comfortable place. Take the SMOKY QUARTZ and place it on your pubic bone. If it has a point, point it up toward your head. Then take the piece of LAPIS and place it over your third eye. Now take the piece of CLEAR QUARTZ and and place it above the lapis on the top of your head. If it has a point, aim it down toward your nose. Breath deeply and feel as if these stones were being drawn into your body like video cassettes are drawn into a VCR. Feel them pulsing and giving out energy. Feel this energy move in waves through your body, resynchronizing and reestablishing your own prime frequency and balancing out your energy body.

You may want to do this for about ten or fifteen minutes once a day for the first week that you try it, twice a day in the second week, then three times a day thereafter. Imagine that whatever feelings and images happen to surface in your mind pass through you as part of the process of healing. Feel, as you lie with these stones upon you, that you're being retuned, back to the song you played before you became addicted. Feel this purity rise up in you. But also feel the ways in which you've grown from your experiences and integrated them into your life. No experience is wasted if we let ourselves learn from it. All healers are wounded at some time in their life. So use the wounds of your addictions to leap out from.

A Crystal Pattern To Support
Your Healing Process

In addition to mental shifts due to chemical addictions, there are definite physical changes that happen when one is addicted to chemical substances. The next crystal pattern is designed to help you move through the healing process, strengthen it, and deepen it in your body. This pattern requires four stones. Two of them, CLEAR and SMOKY QUARTZ, were used in the previous pattern and two are different. You'll want to find a piece of ROSE QUARTZ and a piece of AVENTURINE, a green stone that is also in the quartz family.

For this pattern, the SMOKY QUARTZ is placed in the same position as in the previous pattern. The CLEAR QUARTZ is placed on your third eye. Take your piece of ROSE QUARTZ and place it above your heart, above your heart chakra in the center of your chest. Now take your piece of AVENTURINE and place it between your heart and throat, above the thymus chakra. Lie quietly and feel your breathing. As you inhale, feel that you are drawing energy into your body through each of these four crystals. Feel the energy being charged by the crystals as four strands of healing energy pour into your body.

Each time you exhale, feel that all the physical blockages, damage, pain, and fatigue in your body are being pushed out by your breath, drawn out and released by the crystals. After doing this for a few minutes, if there are specific areas of your body that need healing—heart, liver, pancreas, lungs, stomach—place the AVENTURINE over each of those organs for a while. Feel the same process going on, of healing energy being drawn in and old blockages being released. You may do this exercise as often as you like for as long as you like. After each session, however, you should soak your stones for at least two hours in spring water.

A Pattern to Support Your Growth

Sometimes it's hard to change old patterns: sometimes it's hard to believe that you *Can* change old patterns. One of the problems caused by addictive substances is that they interrupt the capacity to move and grow and evolve. This pattern is designed to help you see and believe in your capacity to grow and change. To work with it you will need three stones: a piece of CLEAR QUARTZ, a piece of

SMOKY QUARTZ, and a piece of AMETHYST that is a tiny bit larger than the other two.

You should lie comfortably to do this, holding the SMOKY QUARTZ in your left hand, the CLEAR QUARTZ in your right, with the piece of AMETHYST on your forehead over your third eye. At different times of the month, at different times of the day, at different times in your body's energy cycles, the AMETHYST will work in different ways. So if it has a point, try it with the point facing up and then down, until it feels right.   Breathe deeply and let yourself think about all the ways in which you want your life to change. Let the feeling of change and joy grow strong within you. Do this for about fifteen minutes.

This procedure will program your AMETHYST to your intentions. Keep the AMETHYST with you. Wear it in a pouch, put it in your pocket or purse or pack. Hold it and rub it, and it will keep recharging you and supporting you in your changes.   If it feels less charged, or if you find that you've changed and need to reprogram it, go through this pattern again.

A Pattern to Support New Life Patterns

Often the process of withdrawal is difficult, and even long after the physical withdrawal is completed, there are emotional and mental withdrawal symptoms to go through. These may keep resurfacing in spite of the work you're doing with your AMETHYST. It's hard to accept the fact that old and new patterns can coexist. If they do, it's common to deny the new patterns and feel that the work you've done to change has failed. The next crystal pattern is designed to help you move through your old patterns more harmonious-ly, so that you don't feel depressed if they return for a while. It is designed to help you take control over them instead of allowing them to gain control over you.

Place your programmed AMETHYST over your third eye, with the point facing down, if it has one. Put your SMOKY QUARTZ on top of your pubic bone, with the point up. Now take a small piece of KUNZITE, either yellow or green, if you can find one, and put it on top of your solar plexus with the striations running up and down your body. Feel that the energy of the KUNZITE connects the new pattern of your AMETHYST with a rootedness in your body facilitated by using the SMOKY QUARTZ. Lie with these stones on your body for about ten minutes twice a day. Breathe deeply and feel that the KUNZITE is discharging your old patterns and reprogramming your will to work with your new ones.

A Pattern to Help You Open up
to New Visions

Sometimes people who have been addicted to chemical substances are so used to the images and feelings and visions that those substances created, it is hard for them to generate visions of their own. As a lot of this book is about learning to work with visualizations, the following pattern is designed to support the process of doing this work. It's hard sometimes to go from watching television, where the images are given, to knowing that you can create your own movies, your own programs, your own images.

For this crystal meditation, you'll need three stones: a piece of CLEAR QUARTZ, a ROSE QUARTZ and a piece of sky blue FLUORITE. Place the CLEAR QUARTZ over the area just under your navel, the area of the energy body which is about sexual energy, and also about intimacy and creativity. Place the ROSE QUARTZ over your heart, to connect loving with creativity. Then place the blue FLUORITE over your third eye, to stimulate a balanced and expansive state of spiritual vision in your life. Feel again that these stones slip into your body like video cassettes. Let them pulsate within you and open you to your inner, perhaps hidden or forgotten, springs of creativity and beauty. Do this for about five or six minutes, whenever you feel the need to open and awaken deeper aspects of your greater self.

Twelve Stones for the Twelve Steps

Many people have been involved in one of the Twelve Step Anonymous programs. These groups have made a great difference in the way people work on releasing their addictions. A major element of the healing people experience through the Anonymous programs comes from working the Twelve Steps themselves. They were designed by the founders of the first such program, Alcoholics Anonymous, tailor-made for the personality and needs of addicted people. The inspiration for the Twelve Steps to recovery, however, came from a contemporary British movement called the Oxford group, which was a path to spiritual growth.

Those of you who aren't in a Twelve Step program would find it useful to read the A.A. book, *The Twelve Steps And Twelve Traditions*, available at almost any Anonymous group meeting and often at the public library. (It is familiarly known to members as The Twelve and Twelve.)

There are tools that can be worked with as you move through the Twelve Steps that can deepen the experience of each step and support you in the process of release. For each step, there is a crystal you can work with. As you begin the step, hold the crystal between the palms of your cupped hands and read the words of the step out loud several times until you feel that the information for that step has penetrated into the crystal. If you have a copy of The Twelve and Twelve, you might also hold the crystal as you read the expanded explanation in the chapter corresponding to that step. Then keep the crystal with you, in a pouch around your neck or in your pocket, as you move through the step. Remember that working with the crystal will potentiate each step, so if your experience of that step becomes too intense, you may want to put down your crystal for a while.

In the FIRST STEP, you admit to your powerlessness over the addiction and the ways that your life has been become unmanageable. The crystal to work with when doing this step is AMETHYST. It helps bring clarity and honesty to the mind and supports the process of being ready to make changes in your life. You don't need a large crystal. A piece about an inch long will do, but if you are drawn to a larger piece then by all means use it.

In the SECOND STEP you come to recognize that a power greater than yourself can rebalance your life. A crystal to work with when moving through this step is light green TOURMALINE. The soft, cool greenness of this stone draws in a strong and loving healing energy that can help to awaken this sense in our conscious minds.

STEP THREE invites you to turn your life over to the care of this power. An excellent stone to work with is pink TOURMALINE. It channels energy to us as light green TOURMALINE does, but the pink color it carries is nurturing and supportive and full of universal loving.

In STEP FOUR, you are asked to make an inventory of yourself. CHRYSOCOLLA, a beautiful turquoise stone, is an excellent tool to use when working this step. It helps to open the inner eye so you can see yourself clearly. But it does it in a compassionate and healing fashion that leaps beyond guilt and blame to a simple admission of who you are and who you have been.   In doing so, it also supports your capacity to grow into who you can become.

STEP FIVE encourages you to admit the nature of your wrongs. MALACHITE is an excellent companion to work with when doing this process. It will bring to the surface all the hidden guilty places, so that you can see them clearly, in spite of how difficult that usually is.

The SIXTH STEP signals a readiness to release all of your character defects. Light blue FLUORITE, especially a fluorite octahedron, is a wonderful tool to be with when you are working this step. Blue like the sky on a clear and beautiful day encourages you to become clear and beautiful yourself.

STEP SEVEN has you turn to the greater power and ask It to remove your shortcomings. ROSE QUARTZ is the tool to work with in this process. The energy ROSE QUARTZ connects you with is love. What better source to turn to for healing than love, and what better energy to cleanse and renew you?

In STEP EIGHT, you are encouraged to make a list of all the people you have harmed and become willing to make amends to them. This is hard work. It requires honesty and strength. A tool to work with on this step is CARNELIAN. Its red-orange color will connect you to the energy of the earth in a grounded way that will support this new way of relating to others.

In STEP NINE you make ammends to people you have harmed where ever possible. The stone to work with is AVENTURINE which helps you to move energy freely through the heart center and begin to repair relationships.

In STEP TEN, you continue your inventory, generally on a daily basis, and learn to admit your wrongs. It's hard to be this honest with yourself, and hard to learn to be honest in the moment. By working with CITRINE QUARTZ, you bring the golden warmth and radiance of the sun to your dark inner places and begin to develop the strength to be honest at all times, with others and with yourself.

In the ELEVENTH STEP you deepen your connection to Spirit so that you move with It as It moves through you. CLEAR QUARTZ is a lovely tool to sit with in your prayers and meditations, to carry with you as you move toward Spirit to embrace It and be embraced by It.

In the TWELFTH STEP, having experienced a healing and spiritual opening through the previous steps, you are encouraged to use the steps in every part of life and to share them with others who might need them. For this final step, a powerful friend to work with is pink KUNZITE. This stone is a strong one. It channels a powerful energy of healing and love through its pinkness, and will be supportive in your life and in the world as a healer inviting others to remember that they are healers too.

What If You Cannot Afford Crystals?

Crystals are among the most powerful and beautiful of this planet's healing tools. However, if you live in a place where the different stones we mention are not available, or if you cannot afford them, don't feel you cannot work with them. The energies of each kind of crystal are distinct and resonate like radio and television waves do. If you're old enough, you may recall that the earliest radios commonly available to the public were crystal sets. So, with a little practice, you can tune into their wave length, the same way a radio or television receiver tunes into the wave lengths of various stations.

Many healers who work with crystals, in fact, outgrow the use of stones on the physical level and continue to work with them on an energy level, by creating large stones in their mind. You also, at times, will want to work with these energies in ways you could not if they were only physical. Some of the stones you might like to work with are too costly or too rare, or you might like huge boulders of them. Ultimately, as we evolve spiritually, we'll all be able to do this, and we'll let our crystal friends return to their own continuing, albeit imperceptibly slow, evolution toward more and more beautiful, pure jewels.

How can you learn to tune into the frequencies of the stones on a nonphysical level? You can pick up the frequency by meditating with a photograph of the stone, by looking at it in a museum, or by holding it in a store and carrying home a mental replica of it even though you cannot buy it. By tuning into it, you can memorize the feeling and duplicate it whenever you need it, so you can work the exercises in this chapter with your invisible but present etheric stones.

By now you've probably begun to learn how powerful visualization can be. Try visualizing crystals—see yourself holding them, drinking in their colors, and learning to work with them. Create a chunk of ROSE QUARTZ in your hand and merge with its energy. Then create a piece of TURQUOISE and feel how different it is from ROSE QUARTZ. It's nice to have the physical stones in your hands, but it's also useful to know how to create them.

There are other healing ways to use visualized crystals that go beyond what we can do with solid stones. Try meditating and creating a crystal so big you can comfortably and safely sit inside it. Let yourself feel how empowering that can be, as you conjure up a stone whose energy or color you feel you need. Or put a giant crystal around yourself at work, and see how that can change your mood, your power of concentration, and your energy level. When you get home, you might want to slip into a liquid crystal bath, which you've created in your mind. You can make a bath out of any stone you want to. You can enclose your bed, your desk, your room, or even your entire home or workplace in an enormous crystal. Crystals are wonderful power tools—but the mind is more powerful still. In the future, as we develop the power of the mind even further, we won't need to use physical crystals except in preschool and kindergarten.

CHAPTER FIVE

CLEANSING THE BODY OF ADDICTIONS

The Importance of Body Work

There are many ways to cleanse your body as you recover from your dependency or addiction. We're so accustomed to thinking of the healing process as verbal, as counseling and therapy, that we forget the ways in which the body also needs its own healing. Often addicts who have been in Twelve Step programs, therapy, or talk groups, seem to reach a point beyond which they don't continue to grow. Often that is the point at which body work becomes the next step. We forget that the body carries memories of pain, fear, and sorrow. We forget that toxins are carried in the body from substance abuse long after the addiction itself has stopped. We forget how stressful life is on the body, even without being an addict. We forget that we're fourfold beings, focused in our bodies and experiencing the world through them.

Rest, Relaxation, and Exercise as Primary Healers

Physical rest is an important element in physical healing. Addiction is stressful to the body. Many addicts are so used to high stress levels that they approach their healing with the same force. It's necessary to slow down sometimes and let the healing process take as long as it takes. Everyone wants to get better overnight, but it probably took years for you to become an addict, and it may take years to heal yourself fully. So give yourself time to soak in a bubble bath with candles burning and soft music playing. Give yourself time for a long walk through the park. Don't feel guilty if you're not doing something every waking moment to get well again. Part of getting well is opening yourself to the body's natural cycles of activity and rest, of movement and relaxation.

Animals understand this. They sprawl out in the sun and melt. But if a bird flies by, or a squirrel leaps over the fence, a dog or cat is up in an instant, alert and moving. Yet a minute later, when the bird flies off, when the squirrel scampers out of sight, that dog or cat collapses back on the grass again, luxuriating in the pleasure of the moment. We too can be like that—as capable of relaxing as we are of moving. Our world is so work-oriented that it's easy to make our healing process a work project too. So it's important to learn to rest, to be slow, to be gentle with ourselves.

Exercise also is important in the recovery process. It in- creases circulation, which carries off accumulated toxins in the body. And it also stimulates production of endorphins, which are natural substances in the body that alter moods, increase   healing, and bring a feeling of well-being. But after a period of addiction, which is stressful to the body, it may not be wisest to go out and start jogging or join a gym. Those activities can   become stressful in their own right. Think about starting to do physical activities that are nurturing and gentle to your body.   Yoga and tai chi are wonderful to start with. There are many dance and move- ment classes that encourage a fluid sense of physical self. Walking itself can be healing. You've abused your body, so now find loving ways to use it simply.

How Body Work Can Help

Herbology and acupuncture can be vital adjuncts in your healing process, both during detoxification and beyond. Many clinics are using these modalities now, so you might want to investigate them if you haven't already. Chiropractic care, massage therapy, from Swedish to Shiatsu, and work such as the Alexander Technique and the Feldenkreis Method are useful in rebalancing and cleansing the body.

Most addicts are out of touch with their bodies. You cannot do the kind of damage to your physical body that addiction does when you live in your body fully and love it. Sometimes it takes the healing, supportive hands of a health care practitioner to remind us of our physical selves. People often avoid this work because they fear the flood of emotions that may wash up to the surface of the conscious mind when this work begins. But doing body work brings us to the place where we're ready to ask for help on the simplest physical level, and one of the lessons of healing is to learn how to ask for help.

Often one reaches out to the addictive power tool because one does not know how to ask for help, and alcohol and drugs seem to be saying "Take me. I'll help you." It requires a certain amount of trust to do physical work with a healing practitioner, but it's important to learn that you don't have to do everything for yourself, by yourself. So consider getting massaged and look for a chiropractor—especially one who does nonforce work, and applied kinesiology in addition to standard osseous adjustments.   Explore the world of body workers, herbalists, and crystal healers, not as a replacement for your Twelve Step group or therapy, but as an additional healing tool.

Food as a Healing Tool

Food is another important body healing tool. There are many excellent books on nutrition, and numerous classes are offered on nutrition and cooking. Many substance abusers are also food abusers. Drugs and alcohol alter our sense of what the body needs and when it needs to eat. Part of the physical healing process is remembering to listen to the body and not just the food-craving voice, or the food-denying voice, in our heads. Addiction is damaging to the liver, and as the liver is also responsible for producing the substances that are involved in fat digestion, it's sug- gested that you avoid oils and fats, fatty foods and fried ones that can put an added strain on your liver.

The process of addiction has already brought into your

body many nonnutritive substances. Part of the body's healing will come from eliminating as many additives as you can from your diet, because they put an added strain on the digestive organs. So much of what we eat is highly refined and contains preservatives, coloring agents, and stabilizers. Pesticides are found on our vegetables and fruits. Livestock are fed hormones and antibiotics that end up in the dairy products, meat, and poultry we consume. So try to simplify your diet to the point where you are eating more whole grains, and more organically produced food. Read labels, and remember that the liver, pancreas, and kidneys that are stressed from drugs and alcohol do not need chemical additives; they will heal more quickly without them.

Many people turn to addictive substances because they are disconnected from their bodies and the world. Because they grow underground and are the nutrition-storage organs of plants, we have found that root vegetables are healing, cleansing, and strengthening when recovering from addiction. So add steamed or baked carrots, turnips, parsnips, sweet potatoes, and especially beets to your diet. Fresh radishes are also good, especially the Japanese dikon radish; watercress is also good. And teas can help. Chaparral, sassafrass, and wintergreen are good, but let your intuition lead you to what's best for you. A cup once a day is enough. You don't need to be compulsive about it. Take the food or tea into yourself, saying "I take you in as a cleanser, I take you in to heal me."

As you begin to eat more fresh foods, whole grains, and beans, your digestive tract will experience shifts in functioning. You may find yourself more gassy and having more frequent bowel movements. These foods may also initiate a healing crisis in your digestive organs, as old toxins are released. The more slowly you eat, and the more you chew your food and avoid drinking during your meals, the more you will support your body as it moves through these changes.

You've been putting unwholesome things in your body for a long time. Now it's time to honor your body and only put healing substances into it. Try to listen to your body-voice so that you eat when you're hungry and not when you're anxious, upset, and in need of comfort. Listen to your body needs and respond to them. Sit quietly for a moment and turn to your stomach and ask it what it needs, rather than deciding with your head or just with your eyes. Our tongues are excellent monitors for body needs. If you're unclear about what to eat, try putting a small piece of food on your tongue and let it sit with you. Feel what your tongue does with the food you've placed on it. Does it push it out or invite it in? Give your tongue the chance to become the spokesperson for your digestive tract and for your body's nutritional needs.

Food is a primary healing tool. It's the building block of our physical structure. Honor the food you eat. Feel that you are part of the web of life on this planet. Feel that what you eat links the Earth and its seasons, links plants and animals, connects you to the farmers, pickers, shippers, and merchants of the world. Know that with each bite you're taking the world in and weaving yourself back into the world again.

EXERCISE: Energizing Your Foods

This is especially recommended for sugar addicts, but also for other addicts as well, as a way to get physically healthy faster. For most of us, except for food we grow ourselves, the life force energy has long since left our food, which is picked, processed, and shipped long before we eat it. Thus, it is helpful to channel energy into our food in the form of light or healing energy. Much of the water we drink is polluted. If pure water isn't available, doing this exercise will help to energize and purify your water.

1. Put yourself and the food in a bubble of white light.

2. Hold your hands above the food, and direct a current of light or energy to flow from your Core Self through your hands and into the food. You may find it flows more naturally from one hand or the other. This is not a matter for concern.

3. Imagine the light surrounding and penetrating the food. Also light up your digestive system and brain. (It helps some people to look up a drawing of the digestive system.)

4. When enough life force has passed into the food, you may feel your hands being gently pushed away.

5. Eat, then dissolve the bubble.

EXERCISE: Centering Yourself in Your Body

All of us have felt at one time or another that we're not centered in our lives. For addicts and recovering addicts this can be a constant feeling. But we can change this feeling by changing the way that we live in our bodies, as our bodies. If we move out into the world from the center of our bodies, from our center of gravity, from our abdomens, then we will begin to feel centered in every part of our lives. The secret to living this way is how we breathe. Most of us are shallow breathers, using only our rib cages to inhale and exhale. But when we're using our abdominal muscles to fully power our diaphragms, then we're working at full lung capacity, drawing more air in and exhaling more waste products from our bodies.

So stretch out in a quiet comfortable place, on your bed, an exercise mat, or a soft rug. Close your eyes and with one hand lightly massage and explore the other hand and arm, then switch hands and explore the other side. Take both hands and reach down to explore one foot and leg and then do the other side. Now move to your head, slowly feeling your skull, face, and neck. Move down to your chest next, feeling your shoulders and ribs, and reach underneath your body and explore your back. Feel your abdomen now, pressing and kneading with your hands. Feel your body start to tingle with the attention you're giving yourself. Feel your abdomen begin to glow with the attention you're giving it.

Now, begin to become aware of your breathing. Place

your hands over your abdomen and notice whether it's moving or not.   Take several large and deep breaths now. Let your body be like a bellows.   Really stretch out your abdomen so that your diaphragm is drawn down and your lungs fill up completely.   Then really contract your abdominal muscles so that your abdomen sinks in and all the air is forced out of you.   Do this three or four times until the pattern is clear to your body.   Then let your body begin to breathe on its own, continue to breathe from your abdomen.

Notice how your body changes when you do this.   Feel the way your spine rocks as you inhale and exhale.   Feel how this motion in your spine can carry into your pelvis and legs, can carry up your spine into your neck and even your head, so that it rocks a little bit each time you inhale and exhale. Feel the current of breath in your body.   Feel that you are floating on the ocean, and that the rise and fall of waves is the same as the rising and falling in your body.   Feel that you're one with the power of this movement, centered in it and whole.   Feel how deeply you're breathing now, almost without doing anything.

Feel your body relax in an energized way as you release your control and let your body breathe itself.   Each breath you draw in fills your body with energy and warmth.   Each exhalation releases a little bit more of the stored up stress, tension, and toxins in your body.   Slowly you're feeling more and more centered. You're alive in the center of your body. You move out into the world from the center of your body.

Do this breathing exercise for a minute or two each morning when you wake up so that you start your day feeling centered.   Do it again when you're falling into sleep. Throughout the course of the day, stop for a moment and notice whether or not your breath is coming from your abdomen and your chest, or only from your chest.   Start breathing deeply again if you're not.   Remember, you don't have to breathe forcefully, loudly, to breathe deeply, you just have to engage your abdominal muscles again, and you can change your breathing at your desk, on a bus, waiting in line at the bank, or in the supermarket.   Breathe and be centered.   Know that when you breathe this way you increase your circulation, carrying new nutrients to every cell and carrying away waste products. This is part of healing your body, part of healing yourself.

Awakening a Holistic Sense of Self

In beginning to think of ourselves as fourfold beings, we need to remember that there's no separation between mind, emotions, body, and spirit. Western medicine and western philosophy tend to split mind and body, ignoring spirit altogether. But in Oriental medicine and philosophy, there is a deeper understanding of the interrelatedness of these aspects.

For instance, imbalances in internal organs and meridians are believed to cause imbalances in our emotions. So imbalances in the kidneys and bladder may result in fear; imbalances in the liver and gall bladder may cause anger; heart and small intestine imbalances can result in cruelty and emotional dishonesty, when you're laughing on the outside and crying on the inside; while spleen, pancreas, and stomach imbalances can generate a state of worry and anxiety; with imbalances in the lungs and large intestines causing us sorrow and grief. As all of these organs may be damaged in the course of your addiction it's useful to think of this approach as you're working on your healing.

Think of the emotional imbalances you are suffering and see if there's a relation between the effects of your addiction on your body and the emotional outcomes we have listed. You may want to work with acupuncture and herbs to do some of this cleansing. A little bit further on we will be giving you several exercises to assist in this process. But according to Jin Shin Jyutsu, originally a form of body work from Japan, there's a simple way to help create balance in your internal organs and thus in your emotions.

In this technique, we're taught that our fingers are connected to our organs. The thumb connects to the spleen and stomach, the index finger connects to the kidneys and bladder, the middle finger connects to the liver and gall bladder, the ring finger connects to the lung and large intestine, while the pinky connects to the heart and small intestine.

So if you're having problems with those organs or with the emotions that are related to them, all you have to do is wrap the thumb and fingers of one hand around the related finger or fingers on the other hand and hold them for a while. This holding pattern will help to balance you out, and you will begin to sense as you do it how long you need to hold each finger. As a total body balancing it's useful to go through all the fingers on one hand and then the other. For further information on this technique and on Jin Shin Jyutsu see *Jin Shin Jyutsu Is* by Mary Burmeister (copyright 1980) 2919 North 67th Place, Scottsdale, Arizona 85251.

Some Exercises for Bodily Healing

What follows are several exercises that you can use to facilitate the overall healing of your body. The first is a simple sound exercise that can be used to cleanse your body.

EXERCISE: Cleansing the Body with Sound

This is a simple, beginning exercise which should be used throughout the process of cleansing, especially during and after the healing crisis. Lie on your back, open your mouth, and, as you exhale, begin a long chanting of the sound AHHHHHHHH. Feel the sound as if it exists outside your body, enters your body through the top of your head, and then travels through the whole length of your body, leaving through your feet and carrying away accumulated debris with it. If there are specific organs and body parts you want to heal, direct the sound-vibration there with your intention, voice, and through your hands.

This exercise is excellent for those wishing to speed the body cleansing of past addictions, and for those who wish to minimize the negative effects of present addictions. How this exercise works is that the pure sound of AHHH is like an energy broom, sweeping through the person and cleansing the psychic connections between the physical and the energy bodies.

This exercise cannot be repeated too often. Two, three, four times a day or more is fine. The only restriction is not the number of times you do it, but that you should only do it for three minutes at a time at most, with a rest of at least twenty minutes before you attempt it again. Doing it for more than three minutes can overstimulate the passage-ways, rather than cleanse them.

For those with major addictions to alcohol or drugs, it may be necessary to repeat this three or four times daily for three to six months. Lesser addictions, like sugar, coffee, or tea, will probably require a month to a month-and-a-half of daily repetitions. Cigarette addicts should work on this at least twice a day for two or three months.

EXERCISE: Pushing the Toxins Out

This exercise is good for releasing the residuals of the drugs, alcohol, sugar, nicotine, or other chemicals which remains long after you stop using them. It is also good for industrial poisons, side effects of medications, and food additives.

Create the bubble around you. Imagine that your heart is pumping out a green dust rather than blood, the kind of green you see in rich, productive fields. This dust is circulating through all your blood vessels, even the tiniest, healing them of any tension or any residue. It moves through you like a broom, pushing out whatever debris is there. This debris begins to surface, like a muddy-green dust, through all the release mechanisms of your body, through your pores, when you exhale, through your tear ducts, your urinary and excretory system. Keep repeating this until you no longer see or feel the green dust leaving your body; this meaning that your body is cleansed on an energy level.

EXERCISE: Green Vapor Exercise for Healing the Body

Once you have cleansed your body, it is time to bring healing energy to it. The next two exercises are to help you do that.

1. Picture yourself in a white bubble. Up from the bottom comes this incredibly vibrant green vapor like green fields, like the Emerald City. Fill up the whole bubble with it.

2. Breathe this greenness in through your nose. With each breath, feel it filling your body more. Feel it flowing through your blood, until you are glowing green from head to toe.

3. If there are parts of you that remain dark, keep breathing into them this healing green light until they also glow. Feel your body strengthening as you do this, feeling better and better, healthier and more attractive.

4. You shouldn't do this exercise for more than five minutes at a time. You could repeat it two to three times a day if desired. Keep doing it for weeks or however long it takes for the exhalation to be green. If there are body parts that continue to feel clogged and stay dark, move on to the next exercise for a while, and then come back to the green vapor exercise.

Remember what we said earlier, that if you cannot see these things, you may know in some other way—sound, perhaps. Green is vibrant though harmonious sound, but the toxic exhalation is discordant; green may be a hum, the toxins a rumble. Once you have done the healing with green, and feel changed, do the same exercise with orange for recharging, restrengthening, and reviving.

EXERCISE: Cleansing Specific Body Parts

When drugs, alcohol, and sugar are used to excess, they can narcotize certain parts of the body, putting them to sleep so that they no longer perform their usual functions effectively. Stopping the drug may not be enough to rouse these organs from their slumber. Sometimes you have to prod them awake, communicating with them in the language they understand best: light.

Prolonged sugar abuse, for instance, may put stomach walls and intestines to sleep, so that they are unable to metabolize food properly. Thus, even though you change to a healthy diet, you may not be getting much nourishment from what you eat, and the resulting starvation may drive you back to sugar. By communicating with the stomach, liver, pancreas, and intestines, however, you can get the nourishment you need, avoid that feeling of starvation, and get healthy sooner. Alcohol addicts often have similar problems with these organs, since alcohol contains a strong concentration of sugar and also acts directly on these organs as an anesthetic. In addition, addiction has a profound effect on the endocrine system, on the glands—pituitary, pineal, thyroid, thymus, and others. Recently, it has been discovered that the heart has endocrine functions also. So be sure that you tune into the glands.

If you're aware of specific organs which were damaged during your addiction, use the following technique to speed up the healing process. Sugar addiction affects the stomach, pancreas, liver, and intestines directly; it affects the heart and brain less directly. Alcohol has an anesthetic effect on the entire body, but especially affects the liver, digestive tract, brain, and heart. Toxic residues of other drugs may be stored in the liver and brain. Cigarettes obviously affect the lungs, but so do marijuana and hash.

1. Identify the body part or parts you wish to work on. (One at a time is best.) Find pictures of that organ and familiarize yourself generally with how it works. (The public library should have some simple explanations if

you do not own any books on the body.)

2. Place yourself in a bubble. Call on your Core Self to help you, since it constructed the body and knows exactly how to repair it. Work until you feel a strong connection.

3. Fill your bubble with a rich orange light. Place your hands over the area you wish to heal and inhale the light directly into it.

4. Feel the organ itself begin to glow with orange light. Talk to it and tell it to wake up, that you have stopped taking in the substance that harmed it, and that you intend to take better care of it in the future. Express your appreciation for the service it performs for you.

5. Intensify the light in that organ, visualizing it working perfectly.

6. If you're taking any medication, herb, or vitamin to heal it, let your body know that this substance is a gift from you to help it get well. (Each time you take in that substance, light up both it and the organ, reminding your brain and the organ what it is for.)

7. If the digestive system is involved, repeat the process each time you eat.

On Physical Pain

There's an aspect of physical healing we haven't mentioned yet, and that is physical pain. This is often connected to mental and emotional pain, which we will be working with in other chapters. Often, however, the physical pain itself is so intense, we cannot begin to deal with anything else. Many addictive substances cause physical damage that may result in pain. There are also many secondary causes of pain well known to many addicts: the fall down a flight of stairs you took that night you were stoned out of your mind, the whiplash and broken bones you suffered from the automobile accident you caused when you were driving home intoxicated.

If you're suffering from physical pain, the work of physicians and other healing professionals is required. But there are spiritual tools you can also use to deal with the pain. Pain-killers of various kinds have been used for thousands of years and have brought great relief to many sufferers. But many of them are highly addictive and many people's addictions may have begun with taking them. So if your pain is manageable without taking them, or if you're on pain-killers but know about the added power of this kind of work, try the following exercise.

Pain is like a smoke detector. It buzzes to tell us that something is on fire somewhere and needs to be taken care of. If we deny the pain, we'll ignore the fire until it may be too late. But most of us try to block out the pain, withdraw from it, tense up and try to feel stronger in order to protect ourselves from it. But pain is a teacher, and in this exercise we will be studying with it.

EXERCISE: For Being with Your Pain

1. Create the bubble around you. Fill it with a rich coral light. Become aware of your breathing now and become centered in it.

2. Begin to experience your pain as a shape, size, texture, color, temperature, and smell.

3. When this sense of your pain is clear, turn to it and talk to it. Ask it why you have it, what it came to teach you, and the kinds of things that you can do to learn the lesson so that it can begin to go away. Words, feelings, or images may rise to the surface. Don't be afraid of them. Keep breathing and be aware. Try to honor what the pain is telling you.

4. Now begin to feel that your body is as porous as a sponge. Each time you inhale, feel that you can draw breath and the coral light directly into the pain itself.

5. Each time you exhale, feel that you can shoot some of the pain out of the top of your head, the tips of your fingers, or the bottoms of your feet, depending on which part is closest to it.

6. Gradually begin to feel that the shape and intensity of the pain is diminishing, as you repeat this exercise and begin to make use of the information the pain is giving you.

7. Dissolve your bubble when you are done, but carry some of the coral light with you. And repeat this exercise whenever you need to.

Essences and Stones to Help in Cleansing the Body

The flower essences do help heal physical ailments as well as emotional and spiritual ones. The essences work on mind, body, and spirit, so there is not exactly a strict one-on-one correspondance between a remedy and a physical ailment. Rather, in the course of taking a remedy for a emotional or spiritual problem, the physical ailment related to that dis-ease improves.

However, certain of the flower essences are clearly related to physical healing. CRAB APPLE is a bodily cleanser as well as an antidote to self-disgust. SPRUCE is said to be excellent for the detoxification process. APRICOT and BANANA are extremely helpful to the hypoglycemia that often arises from addictions to sugar, alcohol, and caffeine. IMPATIENS not only helps with emotional irritability but with any irritation in the physical body as well. SELF HEAL is a general stimulant for the body/mind capacity to heal itself. EUCALYPTUS is helpful for the lungs, as well as for the grief that often underlies lung damage. In the book, *Flower Essences And Vibrational Healing,* by Gurudas, much more information is given on remedies which ease damage to specific parts of the body.

There are certain crystals that can help you in healing your body. You can work with stones that are pink or orange or green to support the work you do with the color visualizations we have shared with you here. ROSE QUARTZ, CARNELIAN, and AVENTURINE are all excellent healing tools. Black TOURMALINE is useful for assisting the body in releasing negativity and toxins. BLOODSTONE is a good support for cleansing the internal organs. There are many excellent crystal healing books and courses which will give you more specific information on using stones to heal your body.

Healing the Body with Love

Ultimately, the greatest healer of all is love. We have all grown up in a culture that devalues the body as being dirty, impure, as a prison for our spirits. At the same time, it tells us that this is the only life we live, and we have to be as healthy and beautiful as possible in order to be good people.

It's hard to live in our bodies with that ambivalence. In addition, many addicts have come to their addictions because they feel detached from their bodies, hate their bodies, have been abused or injured or wounded physically. How many of us are hooked on diet pills because of the way that we feel about our bodies? How many of us returned from Vietnam as addicts? How much alcohol is consumed to wash down the fear and loneliness and sorrow of abusive families and marriages? Ultimately, love is the greatest healer of all, and we're all looking for it. We hope to receive it from someone else, from a parent or lover. But sometimes we have to start with loving ourselves and tapping into love ourselves. When we do this, our lives change. We then bring a great healing to our bodies.

1. Create the bubble around you. Make it as radiant as

you can.

2. Feel that there is a giant pink sun outside of your bubble shining high above your head. Warm rich waves of luminous pink light are pouring forth from this sun, warming you, filling your bubble with pinkness.

3. This sun is the essence of pure love, its light is pure love. Let your bubble fill with this light, let it wash into your body and fill you until your skin, muscles, nerves, internal organs are all bathed in this same rich pink light and are all glowing brightly.

4. As you're filled with this light say these words to yourself, over and over again. "I am filled with love. I become love. I love myself and I love every part of my body."

5. Know that your heart is the storage tank for love. As you slowly dissolve your bubble and return to a normal state of waking consciousness, know that a spark of this pinkness is in your heart still, and will always be there. Whenever you feel lonely, whenever you feel detached from your body or disgusted with it, repeat this exercise and remember that the giant sun above you and the little sun inside are the same. So find love within, and be love.

The Many Levels of Physical Healing

What we know about the universe comes to us through our bodies. Part of the healing of addictions is a physical healing. But as addiction is not an isolated matter, physical healing is not either. It may involve your working with doctors, chiropractors, herbalists, and other healers in addition to doing the work we are sharing with you here. But it is impossible to separate the healing of our individual bodies from the necessary physical healing of the planet we live on.

Earth has been mined and bombed. Its forests have been

so destroyed and its atmosphere so polluted that the very air we breathe is an endangered species. Rain forests, the lungs of this planet, for example, are being cut down to provide grazing land for our fast-food beef cravings, while edible plant proteins are neglected.

It will do us no good to heal our bodies and our lives only to take them out into a world that is dying. Part of the process of physical healing, part of ending the self-directed patterns of addiction, is to get involved in whatever way appeals to you to work for planetary healing. The energy you give to our damaged home will surely come back to you in better air and water, better food. For in the end, there is no more separation between our bodies and the body of the Earth than there is between our spirits and the Spirit that includes us all. And there's no real separation between the healing we make in one place and that which goes on in the other.

CHAPTER SIX

CLEANSING THE EMOTIONS

The Predictable Emotional Crises of Recovery

Once you have stopped using the substance, you are on a long path to recovery. Although every recovery is different, just as every individual with an addiction is different, there are some common traits and issues that many have to face. When the substance is the same, many of its effects on the mind, body, and spirit are quite similar. That is why people in various Twelve Step recovery programs are so able to identify with and help one another. In the course of healing yourself, there are certain predictable crises in which particular long-suppressed emotions come to the surface in a rather large dose. Among them are anxiety, anger, and guilt. You cannot predict exactly in which month of sobriety or abstinence they will come up, but you can expect that at some point they will.

We will look at these crises in some detail, because recovering addicts need help in mastering them in order not to relapse or to switch to another addiction as a means of running from the feeling. The flower essences are a great gift to the recovering person, for taking them helps in cleansing these accumulations of emotions and also in learning new ways to cope with similar feelings in the future. In addition to the essences which apply to each crisis, there will also be affirmations and healing meditations using light. The combination of the essences and light is especially powerful in cleansing and healing these accumulations of emotions. Thus, if you have the remedies for the particular sets of emotions you are working on, you will want to take the drops directly before doing the exercise, to enhance the work.

Understanding the Emotional Cleansings

The remedies and exercises discussed in the remainder of this chapter are designed to clear out emotions which have been stored up in the body and mind through the years of addiction and even before. The substance was used to deaden the unwelcome emotions, to numb the consciousness, and yet all it really did was put them on hold. The part that got frozen lived on in suspended animation, and as more and more of it accumulated, emotions became more and more fearsome. One of the things that will happen as you recover—whether through the process in this book, through self-help groups, through therapy, or even in stubborn solitude—is that those frozen emotions will thaw out, and you will have to experience them. They will thaw out as gradually as you need, and only as you are truly ready to deal with them.

Since the thawing out is part of how you get well, never make the mistake of blaming the feelings that come up in this process on your therapist, on A.A., or any other support system. Without these supports, the feelings would come up anyway, but you'd have less help in understanding and dealing with them. What the remedies and exercises in this section can do is speed up the healing, because they are power tools for transforming the emotions in a way that talking never can. They bring the emotion to light, so that you may temporarily see it with blinding clarity and then experience it, but with a new enlightened perspective and with tools to resolve it.

If feelings come up strongly, continue with the particular exercise or remedy or work with chakra cleansings in the same color light as the exercise. Several essences work more generally on cleansing and integrating powerful emotions—CHAPARRAL, FUSCHIA, and SCARLET MONKEYFLOWER. If you are too overwhelmed, once more read the section on the healing crisis and the rules for healing, and follow the recommendations there. Work with only one emotion in a week. Congratulate yourself on having the courage to tackle that feeling and on your determination to get well.

Anger, Resentment and the Crisis of Rage

Many addicts are rageful people, and one healing crisis you'll go through at some stage is the crisis of rage. That is not to say that addicts have more anger to begin with than the average person, but it is poorly managed, out of fear of confronting or expressing it—fear which we acquired as children and which our culture reinforces. There is also anger at the self about being addicted, and anger at the world for not understanding, for not protecting them or making it better.

Many addictive substances also irritate the nervous system and damage the chakras, and there is contagion from the physical irritation to irritation at the world and people around us. Alcoholism, in particular, both stems from and creates a problem with regulating anger, so that the liver, the spiritual center for discharging anger, becomes a swamp of mismanaged anger.

The substance is often used to dull the anger. Sugar, for instance, can transmute anger to depression. But some substances, such as alcohol, are also sometimes used to let out the accumulated rage explosively, inappropriately, dangerously. There is relief from the pressure of the rage, but at a high cost to relationships and to the body. Guilt and isolation ensue, and then the person may drink, eat, and take drugs even more to dull those unhappy feelings.

The truth is, addicts can ill afford even justified anger, because there is such a tendency to eat, drink, or take drugs as a result. Rage and resentment also damage the physical and energy bodies—it's like trying to keep lightning in a paper bag. The best thing to do is to release it immediately, whether justified or not, in a nondestructive way like the remedies and exercises to follow.

A major task for the addicted person, is to get rid of the backwater of accumulated anger and resentment. The remedies and exercises which follow are designed to do that. Use them in the course of a week, and if you find yourself physically tired from them, get extra rest. Memories of anger-producing incidents may surface. Don't vent the anger inappropriately on those around you.

The crisis of rage comes eventually to all addicts, drunk or sober, as the chakras break down or get repaired. It is not caused by the remedies and exercises. It will come at the point in your recovery when you are ready for it. You are in the crisis if you find yourself walking around angry for days at a time, if everything and everyone around you annoy you, and if you find yourself wanting to strike out physically at the slightest provocation. If this happens, don't get freaked out by it. By this large response, you are demonstrating your readiness and ability to give up a large amount of anger all at once. You will never release more anger than you are able to handle—you are not about to become a maniac.

The greatest problem during this crisis is your own fear of anger. If you weren't taught early on to be terrified of anger, to stuff it down with one substance or another, then you wouldn't have stored up so much in the first place. You were taught to run from anger, so your primary response to the crisis of rage may be the desire to run—possibly to run back to your addiction, since that was for so long the prison guard of your rage. Recognize the drink thoughts, the drug desires, the food pulls, as fear and as conditioned responses to rage. An excellent book to read is Theodore Isaac Rubin's *The Angry Book*, particularly his chapters on how anger relates to addictions and to self-hate.

What you need is another way of responding to rage, a safe and nonaddictive response. Get physical release by running, swimming, or beating your bed with a tennis racket, all the while surrounding yourself with a bubble of white light. Know that the power of white light will transmute the anger more quickly. Treat yourself tenderly. Do not go at this healing in the same addictive way you went at everything else in your life. It took decades to store up all that anger and resentment, so don't think you have to get rid of all of it in a week. If you are getting a massive response—and not everyone does—then only do an anger or resentment exercise once a week. The rest of the time, you could relax and do something for pleasure, strange as that may seem.

Once you have done this cleansing, you may find that certain areas of your life have inexplicably changed for the better. You wind up having more physical energy, more initiative and self-assertiveness, and you get relief from depression and better sexual and love relationships. From time to time, however, you may need to go back and repeat them. No matter how healthily self-assertive you may become, there are still anger-producing circumstances in our daily lives that we are powerless to do anything about. We get jostled in crowds, the train is stopped in the tunnel, the dog next door barks all night. These situations can cause new residues of anger that we need to release periodically.

Remedies Which Help With Anger

BEECH is for intolerance and irritation with others' faults; CHERRY PLUM helps develop self-control in those who are prone to violent eruptions of temper; IMPATIENS eases impatience and irritability; MIMULUS, in combination with some of these remedies, can help those who are afraid of anger; SCARLET MONKEYFLOWER is for integration of strong emotions; TRUMPET VINE helps develop self-assertiveness; VERVAIN is good for those who become incensed at injustices.

EXERCISE: For Specific Angers

1. Sit in a bubble of white light. Create outside your bubble, at the solar plexus, a little ball of red light. It's a magnet and a repository for anger.

2. Visualize that the anger leaves you and travels to the red light. You can do it with a specific incident you're angry at. Remember the incident, feel the anger, and shoot it into the red ball. If it is a person you're angry at, it still works. You're not trying to get rid of the person, just the anger.

3. When you've projected all the anger out into the red bubble, fill up your own bubble and body again with white light, energize it, and breathe it in. Project it out your body to the red ball, knowing that it is the energy of love.

4. As the white light reaches the red light, it mingles with it and slowly turns it pink. Watch as the pink ball slowly vaporizes and disappears, or send it as a gift to the other person or to a place where love will do some good.

An alternative is to focus on generalized anger stored in the body, perhaps accumulated through the course of your lifetime. Surround yourself with the sphere of light, and as in the earlier part of this exercise, visualize a small red bubble at the level of your solar plexus, outside your own bubble.

Focus on the anger stored in your body. If it's in your head, say "Anger that lives in my head—leave." Feel it shoot out of your heart. Feel it pulled toward the red bubble and sucked in. Do so with anger stored in the neck, stomach, back, anywhere. Shoot it outward. (Anywhere in your body that you've ever had an infection or inflammation, you can bet anger is stored there.) The mouth, liver, and pancreas are often spots where anger gets stored with addictions. When you feel the anger has left you, repeat the end of the exercise as described above, dissolving the red anger bubble into a pink one with the transmuting light of love.

Cleansing the Body of Resentments

In order to heal yourself thoroughly of the painful experiences of the past, you now need to cleanse yourself of resentment. You may wonder whether anger and resentment aren't the same thing. They are, but only in the sense that grape juice and wine are the same. Resentment starts as anger, just as wine starts as grape juice, but once the anger (or the grape juice) ferments and ages, it becomes a new and far more poisonous substance. You drink it again and again, and self-destructive things are done in the name of spite. "I'll fix you. I'll eat at you, drink at you, drug at you."

Even when you've done the remedies and exercises on anger through to completion, you may be surprised at the residues dredged up by the exercise which follows, residues which may be perceived as black, gooey excretions. The only explanation is that, long after the mind and heart have forgiven, the body remembers the resentment and hate on a cellular level. It's at the cellular level, too, that hate can create physical damage—even cancer. Thus, it is crucial to purge the resentment, in order to heal the body and spirit.

Essences Which Help With Resentment

HOLLY works on the very toxic emotions, including resentment, spite, hate, and the desire for revenge. This essence is essential when these emotions exist, as the person may stop their own healing efforts out of spite and self-hate. WILLOW is for bitterness, resentment, and the feeling you got a raw deal in life. DOGWOOD enables you to let go of resentment by opening up to gentleness and grace in relationships. FIG helps in the reestablishment of trust. HONEYSUCKLE can aid in letting go of the past. SHOOTING STAR eases the sense of alienation which so often accompanies an accumulation of resentments.

EXERCISE: Cleansing Resentment

Do the exercise which follows several times for each person you have hated or resented deeply, or for each life situation you have resented. Do it, particularly, for each of your parents and your mate or former mate.

1. Create for yourself a bubble of deep, glowing purple light, the color of grape juice. Envision your body as an empty outline and then fill it up with the same purple color. It may be more effective to envision the body as filled with crushed grapes which glow with light.

2. Now outside your bubble see a ball of purple fire, burning brightly like a furnace, which is to be a magnet for resentment. The height of the ball will vary according to who you are working on. For parents and grandparents, it would be primarily the navel area. For those who may have affected your self-love and self-confidence, the solar plexus is important. (For example, a teacher who taught you that you were stupid, a boss who fired you.) For mates, friends, and other formerly loved people, place it at heart level.

3. Breathing deeply, let your consciousness sink down to the particular center. Then begin expelling the resentment out of that center, from the head on down, instructing each part to let go of the resentment. Freshen up the purple light in the bubble and in your body, and sit in it for a moment.

4. Move the ball behind you and let it magnetically draw off resentments you weren't aware of, which may have come out in distorted behaviors, such as the addiction. Return the ball to its position in front of you.

5. When you have done as much as you can in one sitting, blaze up the purple ball until it is incandescent, and let it spin until you believe the resentment has been consumed. Then let the ball sink slowly until it is miles beneath the surface of the earth.

6. Do this exercise several times for each situation you feel merits it. As long-buried feelings and memories come to the surface during the week, instantly erect the purple bubble around yourself to transform that energy. Above all, do not feel you have to act on the feelings, as they will change during the process. Also do not displace

them on some handy target—your friends, your mate, your pet—but let them stay attached to where they originally came from.

Remedies and Exercises to Cleanse Dependency

Addicts often find it hard to admit to their dependency. Many have spent a lifetime staunchly protesting their total independence yet becoming increasingly more dependent on their drug of choice. This is not independence, but counterdependence, a defense against feeling dependency needs which often went unmet in childhood. Typical of this kind of unrealistic dependency are feelings that you are helpless, hopeless, that you cannot do things, that you need others to do them for or with you, and that without so and so, you'd fall apart. None of these feelings are particularly true of an adult. Our "Cannots," for instance, are an expression of dependency, an attempt to legitimate someone else doing it for us. What you may be calling laziness or procrastination is often nothing more than dependency in disguise. Frequent illnesses that incapacitate you—if only for a day or so—may also be unconscious attempts to get someone to take care of you. As you can see, dependency is the underbelly of many behaviors that go by other names.

In addicts, particularly those whose parents were also addicts, things went wrong in fulfilling their child needs. On an inner level, those needs are still very active and lead to dependency on the chemical or dependency on other people in twisted ways that destroy relationships and cripple the addict's potentialities. Stored-up dependency is part of what made your addiction so potent—you used tools of power when you felt powerless.

When you stop using the substance, the dependency is still there to be dealt with and may indeed rise up full force for a time, trying to seduce you back into the addiction. Prayer and meditation will help, as will working with your spiritual friend, claiming that energy whenever you feel drained and needy. These, however, are stop-gap measures—like a vigorous game of tennis might help if you're angry, but not with the kind of stored-up rage addicts have left over from the past. The rage we will deal with soon, but first we have to deal with unrealistic dependency, since that is often what the rage is about.

The exercises and remedies which follow are designed to drain out stored-up dependency needs left over from childhood situations, when you were too small and helpless to be able to help yourself and the adult in charge didn't nurture you the way you needed. You may need to use them several times over the course of a week. Afterwards, situations may arise in which you experience that unrealistic dependency and see it for what it is. Your neediness may come rising to the surface. Don't be concerned, just keep doing the remedies and exercises, and you'll get clear of it.

At first, some unpleasant feelings may come to the surface—neediness, yearning, pain, or rage. If you do remedies and exercises a second, third, and fourth time, however, this changes rapidly, and just as rapidly may follow changes in habits or behaviors you despaired of getting past. For example, your diet may just naturally change for the better, and you may suddenly find yourself able to do things you've been blocked on for a long time. Temptations to indulge in your major or minor addictions may also be relieved. If the temptations suddenly get worse when you first do the remedies and exercises, take that as a testimonial of how much of a part dependency played in your addiction. Work hard on the remedies and exercises until it passes. Avoid overeating during this time, especially sugar, as that short-circuits the process.

This exercise is meant to cleanse frustrated dependency needs that have piled up since babyhood. We don't need them, we've survived without their fulfillment, and the residue can paralyze us against taking action on our own behalf. Concentrate particularly on cleansing organs related to dependency—the mouth, stomach, and pancreas—or on any organs related to your problem—the liver, if you drank; the area which hurts, if you're ill; your legs, if the problem is that you need to exercise and cannot motivate yourself to do so.

Sometimes in adulthood, we transfer our childhood dependency feelings about our parents onto lovers, spouses, bosses, the sponsor in the Twelve Step program, or even onto our children. After going through these exercises about dependency, be prepared to see more clearly your adult dependency transfers too, changing the words in the exercises to those that are more appropriate to current transfers.

EXERCISE: Finding a Spiritual Mother or Father

1. Get in the bubble and reach up for your Core Self.

2. A few feet in front of you, at the level of your navel, see a silver ball something like the mirror balls at discos.

3. The ball spins, and as it does so, it exerts an enormous magnetic pull on the dependency stored in your body. Start at the top of your head and work downward, allowing the dependency to be drawn out your navel to the ball. As it is pulled out, keep saying, "I release my dependency on ____." (Here insert mother, father, the substance, mate, or any other dependency transfer.)

4. When you've gone through the whole body, let the pull continue, magnetically drawing dependency from the whole body. Consciously, let go of dependency that might be stored in your mouth, stomach, breasts, and lower back. Keep saying to it, "I release this dependency." Move the ball behind you, repeat the process, then move it back in front.

5. When you feel you've done enough, stop the pull. Let the ball blaze up very brightly as though someone put a giant spotlight on the mirrored ball. Let it spin as fast as it can, until it starts to spin apart and dissolves into dust and then completely disappears.

6. Rest in your bubble a minute, taking in the vitality and well-being, the security and shelter of that bubble.

7. Now perceive another bubble in front of you. This is a big, tall bubble, similar in size to your own. Feel it pulsating with energy and love.

8. Allow a spiritual friend of a very high level to enter into the bubble. Sense a loving, nurturing, wise presence. It may be female if you are working on your mother, male if you are working on your father—or you may just allow it to be pure love.

9. Reach out to it with that same familiar feeling of neediness, of the desire to be taken care of, that you have used to reach out for your substance. As you do, a current of energy reaches from your navel to that bubble.

10. From that bubble to yours, along that same current will begin to flow a stream of glowing silver—like glitter, only warm and fluid. It enters through your navel and fills up your body, as much as you can hold, then stops as you soak in the healing nurturance.

11. When you feel soothed and energized by the silver glitter, send it back to the presence out of your navel. Keep one little ball of it in your navel, just as a raja or a belly dancer would wear a diamond. (The jewel was not worn for decoration, we assure you, but for its healing effects on that center. Belly dancers were originally trainers for women about to undergo childbirth.) Now say a loving goodbye to your friend, then open your eyes and rest.

EXERCISE: Cleansing the Father or Mother

We are all androgynous, including both male and female aspects. One difficulty with a culture which calls its divine being "our Heavenly Father" is that the earthly father can contaminate our experience of the divine. If you had a father who made everyone miserable because he drank or was brutal or emotionally distant, then you can have trouble connecting with the spiritual side of life. The cleansing which follows helps you experience the male portion of the divine, the male portion of humanity, and the male portion of yourself in a more benign and loving way.

We live in a culture which utterly denies that the divine being itself is androgynous. Thus, any difficulty with our mothers will only add to our distance from "our Heavenly Mother." So after you have gone through this exercise to cleanse any difficulty with your father and with maleness, repeat it with your mother and with femaleness also. For that, you would use silver light rather than gold.

1. Get into a bubble of golden light and connect up to your Core Self, reminding yourself that it is neither male or female, that you have lived as both sexes many times.

2. Imagine that your Core Self sends down a tube to your solar plexus, a tube which is like a vacuum cleaner. As it vacuums, it removes from your mind and body the negative effects of experiences with your father and other males.

3. When you feel you have done enough vacuuming, imagine that your Core Self now sends fresh and wholesome golden light down the tube into your solar plexus.

4. The golden light travels up your body to the brain, where you absorb a new experience of maleness; it travels downward to your sexual organs, eventually filling your entire body with this glowing light. Let yourself take in so much of the light and energy that you feel full.

5. When you have absorbed all you can, the tube disappears, and the light swirls in your body, giving you a sense of strength, protection, and joy.

6. When you feel refreshed, dissolve the bubble and let go of the light.

Essences To Help With
Parental Problems

GOLDEN EARDROPS gives you a new perspective on childhood traumas and unhappiness, often involving a catharsis of the sadness; POMEGRANATE works to balance out emotional extremes which result from deprivation of nurturance in childhood; RUBY helps with father problems and mends the heart chakra; SAGEBRUSH offsets false identification with parental characteristics and releases you to be true to yourself; SAGUARO eases authority problems related to parents; and SUNFLOWER helps with self-confidence and inner conflicts related to the parents.

Healing the Child You Were/Are

Much of what causes our addictions comes from the wounded child we still carry inside of ourselves. The following exercise is designed to create a healing for you and your inner child, after the work of healing your parents is completed.

EXERCISE: Healing the Inner Child

1. Sit in your bubble. Create a soft pink light inside it.

2. Create on the outside a second smaller bubble. Inside that bubble is the child that you were. You may need to do this several times to create a healing for the child you were at different ages.

3. Feel this second bubble moving closer and closer toward your own until it touches and merges with it.

4. Visualize the child that you were coming toward you, as you open your arms to it and take it on your lap.

5. Feel the soft pink light bathing the two of you together, swirling all around you.

6. Let this child know that everything will be all right, that you will always be with it from now on.

7. Hold this child as you yourself always wanted to be held. Comfort it and tell it all the things that you always wanted to be told that no one ever told you.

8. Hold the child you were close to your heart, so that you can feel your two hearts beat as one.

9. Now release the child to its own bubble and let it return to the past, healed and comforted by a loving friend in the future.

10. Continue to feel the pink light around you until you are ready to dissolve your own bubble.

The Crisis of Anxiety

Addicted people can go through a crisis of anxiety at two separate times in their lives—once in the period known as bottoming out on the addiction. This is colloquially known as "the horrors." Anxiety can strike again in the early stages of recovery, when the lower chakras are beginning to cleanse. Another cause of anxiety is that when you are healing, you're doing two things: you're releasing stored-up negativity and you're also repairing damage. Sometimes the rhythms of the two processes are synchronistic. Sometimes they become unbalanced, and one or the other will become stronger. The added strength of the one seems to push the other away, although in truth the other is also becoming stronger, but we tend not to see this. We tend to interpret the movement away as a loss or failure, which plunges us into despair and results in our throwing the nearer and clearer strand away, giving up, and having to start over. If we can stop this process, and see the growth in weaving-movement, we can rest for a while, and let the healing process continue. In the crisis of anxiety, the person has reached this point and becomes terrified by it.

To focus on the chakras here is a mistake, in that the focus brings up a polarity, a fear that you won't be able to fix the chakras, and that you'll never get better. Do the exercise which follows. The purpose of the exercise is twofold. Initially, you are creating an electro-mental construct that will begin to alter the energy pattern of your consciousness in new, positive, and healing ways. Once the exercise is learned through repetition, once the feeling of calm, bliss, and release is easily achieved—then the bliss is at your command, at the snap of memory's finger, a sort of psychic aspirin to take in other situations of stress, distress, or any negative feeling.

EXERCISE: For Relief of Anxiety

1. Create around yourself a bubble of white light and fill your body with it as well.

2. Feel that your whole body and your chakras are melting. It melts down and becomes a blue pool in the bottom of your bubble.

3. Look into the blue pool and gradually let yourself become as still as it is.

4. When you feel calm again, just dissolve the bubble.

Essences To Help With
Fear And Anxiety

ASPEN is for generalized anxiety and panic states when there is no known cause; BLACKBERRY helps with fear arising from feelings of limitation or lack, especially good in helping you manifest your visions; BORAGE gives courage and confidence; soothing CHAMOMILE brings calmness; CHERRY PLUM helps those who are afraid they will lose control and harm themselves or others; DANDELION helps the nervous person let go of tension; FIG brings insight into unconscious fears, especially where lack of trust is a factor; GARLIC helps with stage fright and performance anxiety, also with nervousness; LARCH is good for fear of failure; MIMULUS works well with visualizations and affirmations for overcoming specific fears; ROCK ROSE is for panic attacks and terror in emergency situations; ST. JOHN'S WORT helps you release conscious and unconscious fears by learning to trust in the divine; and WALLFLOWER is for fear in social and dating situations.

Identifying and Healing Toxic Guilt

Many addicts are consumed by guilt and remorse about past actions, particularly those harmful things done under the influence of the addictive substances. This guilt is poisonous, robbing the individual of self-love and causing self-destructive or self-defeating behavior out of the subconscious wish for punishment. Most poisonous of all, it can lead to readdiction, as the person has a hard time feeling worthy of the love and companionship of other people.

This is not to eliminate the need for making amends to those you have harmed, since that is essential to clearing out the karma of your addiction, but you may need to recognize that a guilt trip is often a power trip. When other people lay a guilt trip on you, it is often for the purpose of manipulation and control—so there may be people you feel guilty toward who have actually been conning you by this guilt/power trip. As you make your list of people you feel guilty toward, evaluate whether this dynamic was in action.

Secondly, when you are on a self-imposed guilt trip, this can also be an implicit power trip of your own. In other words, when you are consumed with an exaggerated sense of guilt over some misdeed or even a thought, you are also exaggerating the amount of power you have over that person. Short of actual murder or mayhem, you rarely have the power to destroy another person. We are self-contained and our souls are indestructible, so you don't have the control or power over anyone outside yourself that you may like to think you do.

Hanging on to guilt, being obsessive about it, is hanging onto that imagined power—letting go of guilt is letting go of the imagined power, so that is why we hold onto it. This kind of guilt is a twisted form of grandiosity, serving to maintain the illusion that we have power over the person or situation. Again, this is not to minimize the need to make amends, just to put into perspective that obsessive and unreasonable form of guilt that causes self-hate.

The purpose of these remedies and exercises is to identify situations and actions the person feels guilty about and then take steps to deal with and heal that poisonous guilt. Thus, do not be afraid of doing the exercise which helps you pinpoint the guilt, because even if there is discomfort in doing so, the succeeding steps lead to release. It is far better to feel a short, acute discomfort that brings healing than to live with unresolved guilt that causes a smoldering self-hatred. This pattern of self-hate is very common even to those addicts who have successfully turned away from their addiction.

By all means, you should get the book *Twelve Step and Twelve Traditions* by Alcoholics Anonymous, if you do not already have it. Though written for alcoholics, the process outlined therein will help any addict, regardless of the substance or habit involved. Relevant to our current topic are Steps Eight and Nine, which deal with identifying the people you have harmed and making amends to them. There is a great deal of spiritual wisdom in the A.A. approach, and those who work the Twelve Steps earnestly go a long way toward clearing out the karma of their addictions. Nowhere is this more true than in Steps Eight and Nine.

Remedies Which Help With Guilt

BLEEDING HEART works on painful emotional attachments which eat at you; CRAB APPLE helps with self-loathing, self-condemnation, and the feeling that you are somehow unclean; HIBISCUS is good for sexually related guilt, as is BASIL; MARIPOSA LILY opens you up to love and heals the feeling of separateness and alienation that so often goes along with guilt; PINE is the primary remedy for guilt and self-reproach; and RED CHESTNUT is for excessive concern and anxiety about others, such that you feel guilty for taking care of your own needs.

EXERCISE: Identifying Guilt-Bearing Situations

This process of working through guilt can generate needless fear and pain if approached without spiritual help. For that reason, you may want to invoke your Core Self as you sit down to work on this exercise. Thus, you are immediately in touch with the part of you that transcends all earthly misdeeds, that has a perspective of many lifetimes, and that can give you comfort and guidance as you embark on the process of forgiving yourself and being forgiven.

You may also call on your spiritualfriend, the one you contacted in the sections on stopping the addiction and finding heart-center nourishment. You should also surround yourself in a bubble of lavender light before doing any of the work and particularly before approaching any of the people you might want to make amends to.

Now make a list of those you may have harmed by your actions and of situations which made you feel guilty. If you can deal with only one or two at present, start with that.

Ultimately you'll want to list them all, no matter how long ago, no matter how petty and ridiculous, or conversely, how monstrous you feel they were. Don't judge their weight—stealing a dollar may seem harmless to an adult, but to a ten-year-old it may be a major transgression which is stored up as guilt in the unconscious even as an adult...the guilt without the memory of how it got there. Don't rush this process or any of the ones that follow. You may need to put it aside and come back to it later as more memories come to the surface. If self-loathing comes up in the process and threatens to interrupt it, blaze up the light.

Just getting it all down on paper is a help—it establishes the parameters of your actual guilt. Many of us have a kind of global guilt that we carried long before we did much of anything to feel guilty for. It may have come from vague past-life memories, it often came from our parents' resentment of our legitimate child-needs, but for many of us it was simply there. Thus, the list helps because you can look at it, know exactly what you did, and do something about it through free-floating guilt in its proper perspective.

Try to understand, with compassion for yourself, what your motives were or what pressures impelled the actions. Moral judgments of yourself do not help and are often too simplistic. The sections on Steps Four and Eight of *The Twelve Steps and Twelve Traditions* and of the *Big Book* by Alcoholics Anonymous are very useful in this attempt to understand your motivations. Once you understand, it is easier to forgive yourself. If you are not a member of one of the Anonymous programs, you can doubtlessly find these books in your local library.

EXERCISE: Cleansing Guilt

1. Place yourself in a lavender bubble and fill your body with lavender light. Draw on your Core Self to help you see your own basic goodness and wholeness.

2. Imagine that the lavender light inside your bubble and inside your body begins to spin like a jaccuzi bath and that there is a drain under your feet where the guilt being drawn out of you by the lavendar light drains away.

3. Place a ball of lavender light in your solar plexus, intensify it and spin it for a few moments. This should help you particularly in reclaiming your self-esteem, which has been damaged by guilt. You may want to do steps 1, 2, and 3 for a day or two before going on to step 4.

4. Again placing yourself in the lavender bubble and lighting up your brain, make up a list of people or situations in your life which have engendered guilt. Remember what we have said about guilt trips and power trips, and consider whether that applies in each of the situations. Also consider the role your addiction played in what happened, and work on forgiving yourself for the addiction.

5. Finally, think about which of your character defects might have been in operation—for example, pride, self-centeredness, a desire to control, grandiosity, defiance, anger, resentment, fear, greed, or a distorted sexuality, all of which are character traits particularly common to the addictive personality. (We have already seen the role of chakra blockage in creating these personality problems.)

6. Know that the remedies and exercises in this section have already helped you prepare for change in each of these character defects. Thus, you know that you are not the same person who committed these acts for which you feel guilty. Acknowledge yourself for working on the addiction and on those character defects.

EXERCISE: Cleansing Guilt in Specific Situations

1. Take one of the people or situations on the list which still troubles you.

2. Place yourself in the lavender bubble and open up a flow of lavender light from your Core Self into your brain. Light up the area of the brain corresponding to memories of that person or situation. It will help if you allow yourself to feel the guilt as intensely as possible.

3. Set the light in your bubble and body spinning, and open up a drain under your feet to flush out the burned-up guilt. Intensify the light as it spins and bask in it for a few minutes.

4. Now stop the spinning and erect a second colorless bubble a few feet away from you. Envision the chosen person or situation in that bubble, as clearly and as in as much detail as possible. Call on the Core Selves of everyone concerned to help in resolving the situation.

5. Energize the lavender in your bubble and make an opening at the heart, solar plexus, or other chakra, whichever feels right to you.

6. Direct a stream of lavender light to leave your bubble through the opening and fill up the bubble of the other person. When the bubble is full, yours is also still full of lavender.

7. Call on both your Core Self and the Core Self of the other person to cleanse the guilt and to help you forgive yourself. Specify how you've changed. If you have not changed or aren't willing to do so, and if you aren't truly sorry for what happened, the exercise will probably not work. Also, if you have resentments toward the person, it is probably best to cleanse your own resentments with the exercises and remedies given earlier before doing this exercise.

8. When you feel cleansed and free of the guilt, dissolve both bubbles.

Additional Feelings You May Need to Cleanse

There are other emotions you may need to work with as you move through your healing process. Many of us carry guilt about our addictions, but many of us also carry blame. In fact, a major way addicted people cope with their feelings of low self-esteem is to project the blame for their habit onto others. We blame our parents, our siblings, our lovers, and spouses for our addiction. If we don't release that, it's impossible to move on.

There is also the problem of shame, which is different from guilt. Try reliving situations where you felt each of these, shame and guilt, and notice how they are different. Shame pertains more to the solar plexus, related to disgrace, dishonor, and losing the respect of other people. It's like children feel when they've soiled their pants. Guilt is a more mature, complex emotion, in which we really care that we've wronged another person, and the heart center is involved.   There's a relationship between shame and blame—when we feel ashamed, we try claiming it was someone else's fault.   Shame and blame, anger and depression, guilt and resentment—these are all pairs.

We need to make a distinction between fear and anxiety. Fear is often the greatest obstacle to healing, and is one of the causal factors of addiction. Many of us are afraid of our own vision and power, afraid or our needs, afraid of life and of change. Our addictive substance may have offered the promise of making us fearless, but it did not work in the end. So we may go through the difficult process of releasing our addiction, but if we don't release our fear as well, we won't continue to change. Often fear is related to anxiety, but they're not the same.

Many of us have been dishonest to ourselves and to others about our addictions and about our lives. We have pretended that we don't have a problem with drugs or alcohol. We have pretended that we're happy when we're suffering. Sometimes we've pretended that we're miserable because that is the feeling we are most familiar with, so that even we ourselves don't know that we are feeling good or happy. We get in the way of feeling better. That is another feeling, that emotional dishonesty in all its different aspects, that we also have to release.

Sometimes in the end of a healing process, another smaller and quieter feeling remains, one that we don't always recognize after all our anger, resentment, dependency, and guilt. In the end it's often sadness that remains. We may be sad at how much suffering we inflicted on ourselves, sad at realizing how much time we wasted. It's sometimes hard to get beyond that sadness, enjoy all that we've learned, and go on joyously with our lives.

Now that you know the structure of the exercise for guilt, you can go through it again making the following changes to work with fear, blame, shame, emotional dishonesty, and sadness. For fear do the same exercise using a bubble of dark green light; for blame create a bubble of yellow-green; for shame use a bubble of mustardy yellow; for emotional dishonesty, create a bubble of a pinkish-orange coral color; and for sadness create a bubble of pale blue light. Or, work with these same colors and do the exercise as you did for anger, creating a colored bubble outside your own bubble that draws the emotion out of you.

Eventually you'll reach the point where through therapy, your Twelve Step program, and these exercises, you'll have cleansed your emotions of all past connections. That does not mean that you'll never feel angry, resentful, dependent, guilty, and so on again. You'll feel all of those things, as they are all a part of life. The difference will be that you'll come to each of them without the stored baggage of the past, so you will be able to move through them more cleanly and easily. You'll be living your emotional life in the present, not the past or deferred to the future. And when emotional surges wash through you, you'll have the power tools at hand to work through them so that you can come back to a place of balance again.

Much of the work we have been doing is about negative emotions and releasing them. There are times when it seems that the negativity goes on forever, that there are infinite layers of it to work through. Part of the imbalance of addiction is an extremism that has trouble accepting the fact that it is okay to feel bad one day and good the next. Addicts often feel that if any negativity remains they have no right to feel good. But we were born to feel good, that is our right. As we do this work, we will gradually clear out much of our old negativity, but until we do that, we need to learn how to feel good, how to feel joyous, how to feel love.

The final step in breaking the bind that negative feelings have on us is our capacity to forgive. We think of forgiveness as something we direct at others, but we have to begin by forgiving ourselves. Without that, we cannot forgive anyone else. We have to come to the place where we accept the past, stop blaming ourselves and others, stop mourning or raging about the ways it should have been or might have been, and start using all that pent up energy to begin transforming our lives.

It's seldom easy to forgive. It's hard to give up the pleasure we get from making someone less wrong, from not taking responsibility for our own lives. It's hard to forgive ourselves too. As long as we don't, we don't have to deal with changing. Forgiveness takes practice. It requires that we see the spark of divinity in ourselves and others. Sometimes it's easier not to see it. Sometimes we don't know how to see it.

The following exercise is designed to help us practice forgiving. It may lead us to taking steps to express that forgiveness out in the world, or it may remain something we do on a spirit level. Know that if the person you want to forgive is no longer in your life, no longer alive, the energy you send out will reach them just the same, and be received in spirit.

1. Sit in the bubble and become aware of your breathing.

2. Let your bubble fill up with beautiful swirls of aqua light.

3. Inhale this aqua light and draw it into your heart, so that your heart becomes an aqua storage vessel, glowing and beautiful.

4. Visualize outside your bubble another bubble that contains the image and feeling of someone you need to forgive. Let your heart be open and feel that you can beam out rays of aqua light from your heart to the heart of the other person. Feel their bubble and then their heart fill up with this aqua light until the two of you are passing it back and forth between you.

5. It is time to forgive yourself. Fill your heart with this aqua light and start to beam it out to every part of your body so that you are entirely glowing in aqua light. Hold it in your body and give thanks for being able to feel it. You don't have to explain now why you did what you did; you don't need to understand why they did what they did. True forgiveness is a courageous moving out from the heart, not the head. It has no but's in it, no halfway points. It is whole and complete and a blessing, even if it is not accepted. You may find that the light does not generate itself the first time you try it, or it may appear but not move. Keep filling yourself with aqua light, and you'll start to feel changes inside you. Forgiveness happens in a moment, but its roots are very long.

An Exercise for Joy

After so much cleansing, there's a time for rest and a time for joy and pleasure. The spiritual elbows may be sore. And now there are all those empty places inside that once contained anger, guilt, dependency, and other negative emotions. So, this is an exercise to do at the end of every cycle, large and small, when you have completed one phase of your cleansing, and are ready to go on.

1. Sit in the bubble, lie in it. You can do this exercise in bed, or you might even want to do it in the tub.

2. Create your bubble around you. Make it as luminous as you can.

3. Fill your bubble up with swirls of rainbow light in every color of the spectrum, visible and invisible.   But especially fill it with the pink of love, the purple of spiritual connection, and the gold of wisdom.

4. Let this light wash into your body. Let it fill every bone, every organ, every cell of you, until you are absolutely radiant.

5. Let this light move into every corner of your consciousness. Let this light pour into all the places you have cleansed.

6. Feel this light beyond the edges of your bubble. First see rays of it beaming out to everyone you have ever known and loved, or hurt, or been wronged by. Feel the same light travel out to everyone. And now feel that this light begins to spread out all through the world.

7. See your self as one point of rainbow light spreading out to cover the globe. You are filled with joy and love and strength and wisdom and peace now. And you see the ways that all the world can be this way. And you see the ways in which you can use your own life to participate in letting this happen.

A Word of Congratulations

You've just done a very brave thing in facing up to your emotions—a thing not only addicts but most members of our culture will avoid at all costs. Perhaps you've spent most of your adult life either escaping these feelings through your substance, or overwhelmed by them when substance-free—or when the substance ceased to work for you. Maybe you felt inundated again when you stopped using the substance. The cleansing exercises in this chapter will help you clear out the backlog of feelings that have accumulated, so that you no longer carry them around with you.

CHAPTER SEVEN

CONCLUSION

A Preview of the Next Book

As mentioned in the introduction, this is a two-volume guide to healing addictions. By working with the material in this volume, you've gained an understanding of the spiritual meaning of addictions. You've been introduced to some very helpful tools to use in your journey of recovery from addictions. You've made a beginning at changing the thought patterns that feed into addiction and relapse, and you've cleansed some of the emotions that may have drawn you to drink, drug, or eat, time and time again. All of this work is fundamental to your healing.

The next book will continue the process. It begins by introducing you to the energy bodies, including the chakras. In order to repair the damage done by substance abuse, the energy bodies have to be repaired as well as the physical body, or you may be subtly drawn back into an addiction. For instance, one part of the energy body involves the heart, and the ability to give and receive love. In the course of addiction, the individual grows more and more isolated, more and more devastatingly alone, with only the substance to fill up the void. Stopping the addiction does not repair the heart's capacity to give and receive love, but the tools you will be given in the chapter on the energy body will help you make that repair. Another chapter in the next book explores past lives and how they feed into addictions.

Especially important are the separate chapters for each type of substance the addicted individual may abuse. Specific information about the nature of the substance's impact on the energy body and how to repair it will be given—for instance, there is a visual meditation for each major substance as well as flower essences and stones. In addition to information on such powerfully addictive substances as synthetic drugs, cocaine, alcohol, and heroin, there are chapters on tobacco, marijuana, sugar, and coffee. There is also information about the spiritual impulse and collective need behind each substance's waxing and waning in popularity. In short, this initial book is useful for healing addictions in general, but the next book gives crucial information on healing the effects of the substance to which you were most drawn. We highly recommend, therefore, that you work with the next book as well.

What If It Doesn't Seem To Be Working?

Stopping the addiction may take longer for some people than others. Don't get discouraged—just trust that it's a process, and that you'll gradually have less and less desire to take in that substance. However, for some there may even be a temporary "worsening" in which you seem to be using more of it than ever.

When that happens know that you're definitely on your way to giving it up—it's a healing crisis of the first order. An inner part of you is saying goodbye to its beloved, wanting to spend all the time it possibly can with it before letting go. Or, the exercises can precipitate an artificial bottoming out, stimulating you to experience, once and for all, how bad the addiction can be. Or, you can be the lion with a thorn in its paw roaring, "I cannot give it up! What will I have if I do?" Trust us, lion, the exercises in several of the sections of this book will take care of the pain in your paw—will, in fact, remove the thorn. And after your paw heals, the substance will lose its power.

Some of the exercises may bring up painful old feelings, it's true, and you may have a desire to drink, drug, or eat because of them. But remember the healing crisis, and know that your courage in doing the exercises is what will get you free of your addiction in the end. If you're doing this process steadily, then when you're truly ready, on an inner wisdom level, rather than on a cerebral level, the substance will just pass out of your life. You may possibly have a slip now and then, when painful conflicts arise during the healing crisis, but don't give it power. Wash the guilt away with the tools given here, and go right back to the exercises.

Just keep on doing the work—even if it takes months to get completely free—because you'll gradually do less and less of whatever it is that you want to be rid of. Don't be obsessive about it, don't worry about it, let go of it. After all, how does someone who's winded after running a block become a marathon runner? It may seem impossible in the beginning, but by running every day, day after day for months, the runner achieves those "impossible" lengths and finally makes the marathon. So will you, if you persist.

Recovery As A Lifetime Journey

It's in the nature of an addicted person to want immediate results. If you had patience to begin with, you wouldn't overuse power tools to push yourself so fast to manifest your life task. No addiction developed overnight. Even the faster acting ones, like addiction to hard drugs, had the seeds planted long before you turned to the drug, and no program of recovery from addiction works overnight. In this program we're talking more about life issues, crucial ones that are not so easily resolved. Thus, it's more profitable to view your recovery from addictions as a lifetime process, a lifetime journey that will be more exciting and more fantastic than any television drama, more exhilarating than any drug...just slower, quieter.

You or your loved one did not get sick with the addiction overnight, and you cannot get well overnight either. Work gently, giving yourself time to heal slowly. To do it all at once would be like coming out of a long, dark hallway into a room you know is filled with treasures. If you turned the light on all at once, rather than seeing the treasures, you'd be blinded by the intensity and see nothing at all. Good explorers light a single match first and look around. Slowly let your eyes become accustomed to the treasures of healing, then turn on the light switch.

APPENDIX

HELPFUL BOOKS ABOUT ADDICTIONS IN GENERAL

The Twelve Steps For Everyone Who Really Wants Them. Minneapolis: Compcare Publications, 1979.

A popularization of the Twelve Steps of recovery used by Alcoholics Anonymous. Valuable healing processes and spiritual growth can be gained by doing these Twelve Steps. Highly recommended. (Publisher has a large list of books on various addictions.)

DeRopp, Robert S. *The Master Game.* New York: Delacorte, 1968.

A classic work of the Sixties drug era, showing how to reach the same state of ecstasy and spiritual consciousness without drugs. He also wrote *Drugs and the Mind*, Delacorte, 1976.

Glasser, William. *Positive Addictions.* New York: Harper and Row, 1976.

A description of various ways to put the addictive personality to positive use. Possible helpful addictions dealt with in his book are running, meditation, chanting, and journal keeping.

Keyes, Ken. *Handbook to Higher Consciousness.* Coos Bay, OR: Living Love Publications, 1975.

Author of several helpful books based on 12 Pathways to spiritual development. He talks a great deal about addiction, which he defines as programming that triggers uncomfortable emotional responses when the world does not fit your desires.

Slater, Phillip. *Wealth Addiction*. New York: E.P. Dutton, 1983.

A perceptive and provocative book about the addiction to wealth that exists in our culture and the misery and destruction it creates for all of us.

Small, Jacquelyn. *Transformers: A Guidebook for the Journey Beyond Addiction*. Pompano Beach, FL: Health Communications, 1982.

A book on recovering from the physical part of addiction through the various forms of holistic health care.

RESOURCES FOR BOOKS AND TREATMENT

Literature about A.A. and alcoholism. Alcoholics Anonymous, , Box 459, New York, N.Y. 10017. Meeting information

Literature on alcoholism and all the addictions. Ask for catalogue. Compcare Publications, Box 2777, Minneapolis, MN 55427.

Books and pamphlets on alcoholism and addictions. An excellent source. Hazelden Educational Services, Box 176, Center City, MN 55012. Also a treatment facility. (800-328-3330)

Adult and young children of alcoholics. (Groups and newsletter) NACOA, Box 421691, San Francisco, CA 94142.

Official literature and information on meetings everywhere.

Overeaters Anonymous, 2190 - 190th. St., Torrence, CA 90504.

BOOKS FOR THE LOVED ONES
OF ADDICTS

Black, Claudia. *It Will Never Happen to Me.* Newport Beach, CA: ACT,1983.

Adult and young children of alcoholics and how growing up with an alcoholic affects them. Cost is $7.95. She is a pioneer in the field. She also did a coloring book for young children called *My Dad Loves Me, My Dad Has a Disease.* It is also available from ACT, Box 8536, Newport Beach, CA 92660.

Fajardo, Roque. *Helping Your Alcoholic Before He or She Hits Bottom.* New York: Crown Press, 1976. (Look in your public library.)

Successful intervention techniques given, step by step. Should work for other addictions as well.

USEFUL BOOKS ON METAPHYSICS

Bry, Adelaide. *Visualization: Directing the Movies of Your Mind.* New York: Barnes and Noble, 1979.

Well-written, simple book on how to create and use visualizations to achieve your goals.

Holmes, Ernest. *Science of Mind.* N.Y: Dodd, Mead and Co., 1982.

The classic work popularizing metaphysics and teaching how to change thought patterns to better your life.

LeShan, Lawrence. *How to Meditate.* New York: Bantam

Books, 1974.

A simple, useful guide to meditation, giving various techniques and step by step instructions. Written by a psychologist who has done objective, scientific research into meditation and other spiritual practices. Author of several interesting books.

Maltz, Maxwell. *Psycho-cybernetics*. N. Hollywood, CA: Wishire Book Co., 1979.

A popular classic on using positive thinking to change the patterns in your life that create unhappiness. Two dollars in paperback.

Montgomery, Ruth. *A World Beyond.* New York: Fawcett Books, 1971.

Author of numerous books on life after death and the spiritual planes. In this book, the spirit guide is Arthur Ford, a medium and an alcoholic during his lifetime. The story of his addiction and its effects on his life after death are told in Montgomery's book.

Roberts, Jane. *The Nature of Personal Reality*. New York: Bantam Books, 1974.

One of a series of channeled books. An exceptional book on how we shape our reality. Highly recommended but hard to fully understand.
Other books channeled by the same author include *The Seth Material, Adventures in Consciousness, The Nature of the Psyche, The Unknown Reality, The individual and the Nature of Mass Events.* Major works available in paperback and in most bookstores.

BOOKS ABOUT HEALTH CARE

Bach, Edward, M.D., and F. J. Wheeler, M.D. *The Bach*

Flower Remedies. New Canaan, Ct: Keats Publishing Co., 1979. (Published in the UK by C.W. Daniel, Ltd., Saffron, Walden.)

The original descriptions of the remedies and their purposes by the man who developed them. Not as comprehensive or understandable as Chancellor's book, but considered the "Bible" on the Bach remedies.

Chancellor, Dr. Phillip M. *Handbook of the Bach Flower Remedies.* New Canaan, Ct: Keats Publishing Co., 1971. (Published in the UK by C.W. Daniel Ltd., Saffron, Walden.)

The best book about the Bach Flower Remedies. There are descriptions of each of the remedies with the purpose and personality traits it is designed to heal. There are case histories about each remedy, including the physical ailments of the person which cleared up as underlying emotional difficulties got better.

Damian, Peter. *The Twelve Healers of the Zodiac.* York Beach, ME: Samuel Weiser, Inc., 1986.

A treatment of the flower essences and their astrological correspondences. Donna's only complaint about this book is that she didn't write it!

Gurudas. *Flower Essences and Vibrational Healing.* Albuquerque, N.M.: Brotherhood of Life , 1983.

A comprehensive book on 108 flower essences, both the traditional Bach ones and newer ones. It has interesting things to say about correspondences between the forms of plants and their healing purposes.

Gurudas. *Gem Elixers and Vibrational Healing, Vols. I and II.* San Rafael, CA: Cassandra Press, 1985 and 1986.

Marie Child, Diane. *Mother Wit: A Feminist Guide to Psychic Development.* Freedom, CA: Crossing Press, 1981.

One of the clearest and most direct books on growth, healing, and expanding your consciousness.

Joy, W. Brugh, M.D. *Joy's Way*. Los Angeles, CA: J.P. Tarcher, 1979.

The journey of a medical doctor suffering from a serious illness through the inner and outer stages of his becoming a spiritual healer.

Gawain, Shakti. *Creative Visualization*. New York: Bantam Books, 1982.

A wonderful book with many visualization tools to use in every part of your life.

Raphael, Katrina. *Crystal Enlightenment*. New York: Aurora Press, 1985.

A fine guide to anyone staring out exploring the world of crystals and how to use them.

Chang, Stephen. *The Great Tao*. San Francisco, CA: Tao Publishing, 1985.

A virtual encyclopedia of information on Chinese medicine, healing, mind/body relations, and energy exercises.

Serinus, Jason. *Psychoimmunity and the Healing Process*. Berkeley, CA: Celestial Arts, 1986.

A book on healing with channeled information, with a focus on AIDS but with valuable information for anyone who has a damaged immune system.

Hodgson, Harriet W. *A Parent's Survival Guide: How to Cope When Your Kid Is Using Drugs*. New York: Harper and Row, 1986.

Far more than that, this book is a clear but thorough guide to addictive substances and their effects.

Chatlos, Calvin, M.D. *Crack: What You Should Know About the Cocaine Epidemic*. New York: Putnam, 1987.

Medical, social, and psychological information that you should know about coke and crack.

Simonton, D. Carl, M.D. Stephanie Matthews-Simonton, and James L. Creighton. *Getting Well Again*. New York: Bantam, 1980.

One of the first and still one of the best books out on using visualization to heal, in this case with cancer, but valuable for anyone interested in the subject.

Gordon, Richard. *Your Healing Hands: The Polarity Experience*. Santa Cruz, CA: Unity Press, 1978.

An excellent book on healing, it leads you through the first steps of awakening the healing power that you can begin to tap into through your hands.

Kreiger, Dolores, Ph.D., R.N. *The Therapeutic Touch: How to Use Your Hands to Help or to Heal*. Englewood Cliffs, N.J.: Prentice-Hall, 1979.

The person who brought healing to the medical world and made it as respectable as it can get right now has written a fine source book for apprentice healers that offers far more on aura and body healing than we could give you here.

BOOKS ABOUT REINCARNATION

Cerimara, Gina. *Many Mansions* . N.Y: NAL Books, 1972.

An excellent and readable books based on the work of Edgar Cayce, defining the principles of reincarnation and giving numerous case examples of how past lives affect this one. She also wrote *The World Within.*

Montgomery, Ruth. *A World Beyond.* New York: Fawcett Books, 1971.

Author of numerous books on life after death and the spiritual planes. In this book, the spirit guide is Arthur Ford, a medium and an alcoholic during his lifetime. The story of his addiction and its effect on his life after death are told in Montgomery's book.

BOOKS ON FOOD ADDICTIONS

Bill, B. *Compulsive Overeater.* Minneapolis: Compcare Publications, 1981.

An overeater's story of addiction and detailed view of recovery through the Anonymous programs. Full of Wisdom.

Dufty, William. *Sugar Blues.* New York: Warner Books, 1976.

Sugar's alarming multiple effects on mind and body, including its addictive properties. Our culture's part in creating a dependency on it through advertising and putting it in foods.

Hollis, Judi, Ph. D. *Fat Is a Family Affair.* City, MN: Hazelden Foundation, 1985.

Ways in which family dynamics and the disease of co-dependency feed into food addictions. A very useful book in terms of making these dynamics conscious.

Orbach, Susie. *Fat Is a Feminist Issue.* New York: Berkeley Books, 1978.

A feminist perspective on the struggle women have with

food and weight, seeing it as a response to women's role in society.

Overeaters Anonymous. Torrence, CA: Overeaters Anonymous, Inc.,1980.

A book describing the O.A. program and the problem of compulsive overeating, with stories of people who recovered.

Rubin, Theodore. *Forever Thin.* New York: Bernhard Geis Associates, 1970. (Out of print, check your public library.)

Excellent, readable picture of the psychology of overeating and the fear of being thin. His best book on the subject. He also wrote *Alive and Fat* and *Thinning in America,* Coward McCann, New York, 1978.

ALCOHOLISM BIBLIOGRAPHY AND SOURCES OF INFORMATION

Alcoholics Anonymous. New York: World Services Inc., 1976.

Familiarly called the Big Book by A.A. members, it gives the workings of the A.A. program and stories of alcoholics who were able to stay sober through A.A. Available at meetings, (many of which are open to the general public), the public library and the resources listed below.

Johnson, Vernon. *I'll Quit Tomorrow.* New York: Harper and Row, 1973.

A classic by a former alcoholic, who is now the founder of treatment programs, giving his own story and the typical course of the progression into alcoholism.

Parker, Ann E. *Astrology and Alcoholism.* York Beach, ME: Samuel Weiser Inc., 1982.

Research into the astrological charts of 100 alcoholics with some preliminary conclusions and alcoholism information.

Steiner, Claude M. *Games Alcoholics Play.* New York: Ballantine, 1971.

Using transactional analysis and life scripts to understand the life script of alcoholism. (Applies to other addictions as well.) Paperback, $2.50.

Steiner, Claude M. *Healing Alcoholism.* New York: Grove Press, 1975.

Having come a long way from his controversial first book, Steiner presents his further learning and holistic methods now in use in his California center for alcoholism.

Youcha, Geraldine. *A Dangerous Pleasure.* New York: Hawthorne Books, 1978.

Women and alcoholism, why it happens faster and is more destructive. Cultural stresses on women alcoholics.

RESOURCES FOR OBTAINING FLOWER AND GEM REMEDIES

The Edward Bach Healing Society, 461-463 Rockaway Ave., Valley Stream, N.Y. 11580.

Source for obtaining the Bach flower essences.

Pegasus Products, Inc. P.O. Box 228, Boulder, Co. 80306. (800-5276104).

Source for obtaining about 700 different flower essences and gem elixirs.